DATE DUE

Demco, Inc. 38-293

Working Mothers Under Stress and their Perception of Spousal Support in the Home

Elysa L. Schwartzman

Schwartzman Publications

Schwartzman Publications

Library of Congress Control Number: 2003093758

ISBN 0-9688966-0-X

ABSTRACT

This descriptive case study attempts to discover whether married working mothers perceive spousal support as related to stress and the presence of role overload and role conflict. A 44-item questionnaire was administered to 20 married working mothers with pre-school children. The questionnaire was weighted in favour of subjective responses based on these women's perceptions of how they manage to juggle their multiple roles (mother, wife, homemaker and wage earner). The collected data were analyzed from two perspectives: analytic and descriptive. The 20 respondents are unanimous in their "satisfaction" with their outside jobs. But when the questionnaire directs these women toward an examination of the domestic aspects of their lives, they contradict themselves. The findings suggest that these women's personal issues related to the problem of balancing workplace responsibilities with domestic and child care obligations are far from resolved. Questions arise: What do these women who "do it all" really want? Has career and financial independence become a higher priority than marriage and family? Carol Gilligan's (1993) relational model of female development and her accompanying image of the "web" provide a framework which may help the married working mother's contradictions begin to make "sense" in the context of modern society.

ACKNOWLEDGEMENT

I am grateful to my mother, who sacrificed so much of her valuable time giving me emotional support as I made my way through this project. Her care and devotion is something I cherish and will stay with me for the rest of my life.

Something to consider before we start . . .

Defining four kinds of domestic labor:

Housework refers to both male- and female-typed tasks performed inside and outside the household (e.g., cooking, laundry, shopping, vacuuming, making beds, repairs, yardwork, paying bills, and car maintenance). *Child care* includes teaching, playing with, and taking care of children. A less tangible type of activity is *support work*, which is maintaining the emotional well-being of family members. The last type is *status production* (Papanek, 1979), which encompasses activities such as entertaining and charitable work that require a spouse's in-home time, energy, and organizational skills and that promote the other spouse's job status. Historically, wives have engaged in status-production activities more often than have husbands.

Shelley Coverman
"Women's Work Is Never Done: The Division of Domestic Labor", 1989.

CONTENTS

Chapter 1

INTRODUCTION

Since World War II, many more women have entered the workforce. Currently, a majority of married mothers are employed outside the home (Lerner,1994). Nearly 873,000 women whose youngest child was under the age of six were employed in 1991; 68% of these women worked in paid, full-time positions - 30 hours per week or more (Statistics Canada, 1992). But women's position in society has not changed at the same pace as their entry into the workforce. The lag-time - the difference between women's evolution and society's accommodation of it - produces stress.

Working mothers in particular are subject to stress from many different quarters. Despite the additional role of working outside the home, women are still primarily responsible for housework, child care and the emotional nurturing within the family. As a consequence, numerous women encounter psychological stress in terms of role overload and role conflict.

Role overload and role conflict, implying too much to do in too little time, are often apparent when a woman functioning as wife, mother and homemaker takes on the additional role of employed worker; role overload is especially predominant in women who have pre-school children (Torjman, 1988; Bird & Wanamaker, 1990; Mackie, 1991). Many working mothers experience so high a level of stress that they feel they have limited control over their environment (Rosenfield, 1989; Lerner, 1994). Both past and current research suggests that men are doing little to ameliorate women's additional responsibilities (Hughes & Galinsky, 1994; Ross & Mirowsky, 1983). Married working women report that a major factor causing them stress is their husbands' failure to assist in household tasks and child care (Hochschild, 1989; Wilson, 1991).

The research question for the present study asks: What is the correspondence between women's perception of psychological stress (in terms of role overload and role conflict) and their perception of support given by their husbands in household tasks, child care, and family nurturing?

The researcher was drawn to the issue of married working mothers with pre-school children because she looked at these women and wondered, *how can they undertake so many roles without neglecting some very essential priorities?* The roles of wife and mother require "full-time" devotion. The role of full-time wage earner demands attention and skill for the better part of each working day.

The role of homemaker consumes all the other hours that remain. How can a woman "do it all"?

Barnett and Baruch (1986) point out that:

> Traditional assumptions about the protective function of the home for women and the stresses of the workplace for men have been challenged by new findings that point to the increased risks for illness and depression in mothers with pre-school children, and the rise in psychological well-being for women who add employed worker to their wife and mother roles. (Barnett & Baruch, in Worell & Remer, 1992, p.51)

In other words, although married working mothers are feeling good about working outside the home, they are also susceptible to role overload and role conflict which they experience in the form of guilt over the quality of mothering they provide, stress arising from the ongoing emotional give-and-take of their marital relationships, and the stress of unresolved emotions within themselves.

Thus the researcher approached the present study with a genuine curiosity as to the limits of a woman's range of accomplishment and her ability to care. Accomplishment and care are the nexus of a modern woman's life. But what are the boundaries? The purpose of this study is to determine how married working mothers perceive the different stressors they experience as affecting their lives and their *sense of who they are*. It attempts to discover whether women perceive spousal support as related to stress and the presence of role overload and role conflict. Ultimately it seeks to offer a "profile" of the married working mother which might prove useful when attempting to address broader and deeper issues concerning a woman's "role" and the expectations attached to it.

Lazarus and Folkman (1984) define psychological stress as, "a particular relationship between the person and the environment that is appraised by the person as taxing or exceeding his or her resources and endangering his or her well-being" (p.19). This definition of psychological stress suggests two things: Yes, psychological stress is immediate in its effect and is becoming an increasingly widespread social problem. But psychological stress is not just a momentary phenomenon; it builds over time and therefore also reaches deeper than the daily grind, affecting the development of that mix of attitudes, priorities and values we call "identity".

Considering this, the researcher approached the present study with the idea that role overload and role conflict - being so directly linked to the phenomenon of psychological stress - might also point beyond the daily flow of job, chores, relationships and responsibilities to the more essential notion of a

woman's identity. The question became not just *how can a woman do it all?* but

why is she trying to? The most obvious answer, simply put, is: for " herself ".

But it seems logical that much of a woman's development must suffer in

the attempt to be all things to everyone - i.e., mother to her children, wife to her

husband, domestic goddess to her family, and a dedicated worker to her

colleagues during the working day. So what are the gains? And what are the

losses? How is a woman with children, a husband, a career and a home to run

able to balance her multiple roles and still see clearly who she is and where she

is headed? In the context of the present study we might well ask: what is role

overload and role conflict doing to a woman's sense of "self "? The researcher

hoped that 20 married working mothers might be able to shed some light.

The literature review in this study traces a range of perspectives on the

issue of the married working mother, from the 1960's and the rise of feminism

through to the present. Carol Gilligan's (1993) relational model of female

development and her accompanying image of the "web" provide a crucial

framework for understanding a complex and increasingly controversial dilemma

faced by women who want or feel compelled to "do it all".

Gilligan's model is based on the notion of human relationship which, in turn, is based on perception. Similarly, the present study's research question is built around perception. Perception, although by definition never concrete or exact, is the better way into a woman's sense of accomplishment, compassion and fairness, *and* her personal limits. Perception also connects directly to the feelings and values that comprise "identity".

Chapter 2

REVIEW OF THE LITERATURE

The Literature Review is divided into two sections. Section One covers a range of articles and books tracing contemporary developments in "the woman's role" as a central social issue in western culture. The readings begin with the rise of post-Baby Boom feminist philosophy and bring us up to current perspectives on how to best approach problems such as unequal division of household labour, perceptions of inequity and care, and gender ideology. As well, Carol Gilligan's (1993) relational model of female development and her accompanying image of the "web" are discussed. Definitions of "stress" and "psychological stress" are also offered in this section. In Section Two, four final articles are discussed which focus directly on the present study's interest in married working mother's perceptions of psychological stress as it relates to role overload, role conflict and spousal support inside the home. Definitions of role overload and role conflict are given at the end of this section.

Section One

Studies done over the years show little change in the life patterns of most

couples (Lennon, 1987; Ross & Mirowsky, 1983). The increased participation

of women in the work force has not significantly altered these patterns. What a

family gains economically from a wife working, it may experience as a loss in

terms of the reduced family nurturing from a wife and mother. In addition, the

conditions of the household itself may have consequences for the psychological

and physical well-being of the house dwellers. As more women enter the work

force, the degree of role conflict increases (Lowe, 1989). Stress also increases

because a woman feels herself to be violating her own as well as the family's

role expectations (Coveman, 1989-a; Eshleman, 1991).

While past studies tend to assume that the unequal division of labor in

working households was a source of stress in women, many current studies take

a different tack and investigate perceptions of inequity as distinct from the

amount of time spent on given household tasks (DeMaris & Longmore, 1996).

DeMaris and Longmore's findings are interesting in light of earlier theoretical

assumptions: "the more husbands agreed that housework should be equally

shared, the less both partners saw housework as unfair to the wife" (1996,

p.1065). Somewhat unexpectedly, "Both partners were less likely to see housework as unfair to women the more hours the later [sic] spent in child socialization activities" (1996, p.1065). Most surprising was "the fact that husbands with more education than their wives were more likely to see their wives as unfairly burdened with housework" (1996, p.1066).

Linda Thompson discusses the concept of fairness in family work (1991). Noting that there is no direct relationship between quantitative outcomes and the idea of fairness, she suggests that "Researchers need to consider valued outcomes other than who does what tasks and how many hours it takes to do family work" (p.193). Thompson recognizes further that although she is "discussing women's personal sense of fairness, it is clear that justice emerges from interaction. Women and men together shape women's sense of what is fair, and it is not simply a matter of women's assertion and men's resistance" (p.194). Perceptions by their very nature seem to be relational. The "experimental" situation in which the researcher observes stress and infers a causal source is at best problematic. When a researcher's findings reveal surprising or inexplicable outcomes, both hypothesis and methodology may have to be altered.

The view of the perceptions and sources of stress for working mothers seems to be changing. Researchers are looking for new ways to interpret and understand the dynamics of key familial relations; perhaps the relationship between husband and wife, among other relationships, is also evolving. The historian Eric Hobsbawm suggests that

> in the developed countries of the world, middle-class feminism, or the movement of educated or intellectual women, broadened out into a sort of generic sense that the time for women's liberation, or at least women's self assertion, had come. (1994, p.319)

Hobsbawm places this great change in women's perception in the context of the social upheaval following World War II. This tremendous and rapid upheaval generated a cultural and moral revolution. "Women were crucial to this cultural revolution, since it pivoted on, and found expression in, changes in the traditional family and household of which they had always been the central element" (Hobsbawm, 1994, p.319).

When Betty Friedan's The Feminine Mystique (1963) appeared, many post war baby boomers were completing secondary school or entering university and mothers had their first opportunity to reflect on a life without children with limited prospects for a job or career. The post war suburban communities that had grown up throughout North America had likewise completed their first cycle. The malaise of discontent and ennui that Friedan discusses in reference to this generation of women is very much of a moment with this stage in the cycle of post war nesting and childrearing. The mother-centered nest, urban or suburban, was a historical and cultural response to the needs of a society whose men (and often, women) had just fought a long, bloody war. The post war family represented North America's attempt to renew itself, even, biologically, to create the next generation. The freedom that many women had experienced during World War II by joining the services or working in factories or at other "male" jobs seemed inevitably curtailed by the society's need to procreate a new generation.

It may be that the fundamental roles women engage in and their perceptions of satisfaction and dissatisfaction in these roles are relative to the historical era. In all times -- and certainly in times of social and economic crisis -- there is less room to make choices than outsiders, including researchers, may perceive. As some of the recent research cited above has shown, both wives and husbands often express satisfaction in relational situations where the researcher's measurement of outcomes suggests inequity or unfairness.

Some of the recent feminist theorists recognize "the need to acknowledge the existence of gender differences in many areas of social life" (Doucet, 1995, p.273). Doucet asserts that it is not the difference between the sexes that is at issue, but who dominates whom (p.274). Rhode states that the questions at issue are " 'not only of gender equality but also of cultural priorities' " (Rhode, 1990 in Doucet, 1995, p.274). Doucet also suggests that insufficient attention has been paid to:

> how women and men experience their changing status as mothers and fathers in relation to a wide range of indeterminate, constantly shifting factors which correspond to the ages and numbers of children as well as to the inconstant (variable) needs and personality of each particular child. (1995, p.275)

For Doucet the problem is the "the point about the difference difference makes and whether gender differences translate into disadvantages" (p.276). The perception of difference whether the researcher's or the subject's, may not in itself be significant.

> In the main, gender differences are viewed as problematic within sociological literature on gender and household labour. While some of these differences may be disadvantages, some are simply differences which are

neither deficiencies nor disadvantages. (Doucet, 1995,

p.276)

Doucet suggests that researchers sometimes ignore the concerns and feelings expressed by interviewed mothers in order to compress those feelings into a category like ideology (p.278). Structuring mothers' responses in this way makes it easier to collate data but also seems "to belittle or dismiss these women's feelings of confusion, tension, and ambivalence about 'a lack of maternal care' as they leave their young children with other carers" (p.278).

Doucet feels that the issue of which perspective one uses to study gender equality and gender difference is crucial. She herself has "found it difficult, if not impossible, to classify couples in terms normally used by authors in this area; such classifications include 'traditional,' 'transitional,' 'egalitarian,' . . . or 'traditional,' 'traditional-rigid,' 'tradition-flexible' and 'renegotiated' " (p.279). The actual relationships between the genders seem to defy neat categorization. Gender relationships are not static and the husband's and wife's view of justice and fairness within their relationship is also not static and may not accord symmetrically with the categories established by the researcher (p.280). Doucet found that "Gender differences in household labour existed for all couples in . . . [her] study" and also "existed within all households, even those whom other authors might describe as fully 'egalitarian' " (p.280). There seems to be a real possibility that the behavioral models and concepts devised by some researchers fail to correspond with the perceptions husbands and wives have about the equity and fairness of their household and child caring arrangements.

Greenstein recognizes that "The key issue here deals with perceptions of justice: under what circumstances will inequalities in the division of household labor come to be perceived as inequities" (1996, p.1030)? Greenstein adopts Crosby's "relative deprivation theory" for his study (p.1030). According to this theory an outcome is equitable or inequitable relative to that of another person, group or past experience (Greenstein, 1996, p.1031). Greenstein's study concludes that traditional wives are less likely to find the household division of labour as unfair and egalitarian wives are more likely to judge it unfair (p.1040). The model types traditional wives compare themselves to, presumably, would be more like themselves in ideology; hence, they would feel less deprived. The reverse would be the case for "egalitarian" wives. It may be that if you label wives by ideology, the outcomes are predetermined. In any event, Greenstein's study does not address the problem of perceptions as raised by Doucet. Perhaps elevating the idea of "relative deprivation" to the status of a theory is to have too high hopes for a construct that can at best aid in gathering quantifiable data from circumscribed outcomes.

Pina and Bengtson (1993) criticize equity and exchange perspectives as a very limited way to view the relationship between the division of household labour and marital happiness (p.902). They hypothesize that "The symbolic meaning of 'help,' with housework as love and support, may be one mechanism linking various divisions of household labor with marital and personal happiness" (p.902). The results of their study are interesting. Their statistics show only "marginal support for the hypothesis that the relationship between the division of household labor and the wife's satisfaction with help and support from her husband would be stronger for egalitarian than for traditional wives" (p.907). However, "wives who are employed full-time have a significantly higher likelihood of being satisfied with help and support from their husband when they have an equal division of household labor than wives who are not employed full-time" (p.907). Furthermore, "a wife's happiness . . . [is] affected indirectly by the division of household labor through the degree to which she perceives her husband as providing her with emotional and instrumental support" (p.910). There seems to be a symbolic value placed on the husband's household labor which is not directly correlatable to any measurable outcome. If perceptions are always relative to other persons or other events and expectations, then it is very difficult to understand them without evaluating them in many dimensions. Pina and Bengtson's study suggests that women who work full-time may have higher expectations that their husbands will share household duties. Moreover, these women may frequently have these expectations realized, possibly resulting in happier marriages.

Perry-Jenkins and Crouter's study of "Men's Provider-Role Attitudes" (1990) serves in several dimensions as a useful complement to Pina and Bengtson's study. In their study "Support was found for the notion that the congruence of role beliefs and the enactment of role behaviors are related to higher reports of marital satisfaction" (p.153). Like Pina and Bengtson's study, Perry-Jenkins and Crouter's is also based on a sample that is largely white and middle-class. In the former study an indirect or symbolic relationship is found between the wife's level of marital satisfaction and her perception of her husband's help in performing household tasks. In the latter study, the husband's evaluation of his provider role corresponds to perceptions of marital satisfaction. In both studies more attention is being paid to the subjective responses of the participants than to the measuring of outcomes per se. Peplau (1983) has "argued that only in examining all dimensions of a role (i.e., affect, behavior and cognition) can we begin to understand the implications of that role for family life" (Peplau in Perry-Jenkins & Crouter, 1990, p.153). An examination of the relationship between attitude and behavior is coming more to the forefront in much of the current research on husbands' and wives' division of household labour.

Some feminist researchers seem implicitly to have epistemological concerns at the focus of their studies (Bhavnani, 1993, p.95). Following Donna Haraway (1988), Bhavnani sees positioning, partiality, and accountability as key elements in any study of the relationship between husbands and wives (Bhavnani, 1993, p.97). Thus the questions of the researcher's position, class and status are important. As in most feminist discourse, it is also assumed that everyone is partial to one or another belief and value system. Finally, accountability seems to translate into the responsibility to engage all the issues (Bhavnani, p.97). Interviewing English working class youths, many of them Black or Asian, Bhavnani examines their discussion of political issues. She rejects any attempt to quantify the data from her interview; instead she charts her awareness of her relationship to her subjects as well as their responses to her and the issues discussed. As is frequently the case in feminist research, the micropolitics between the group and researcher become as much the issue as the subject of politics in England (Bhavnani, 1993, p.101). Not only do relationships constantly change; the relativity of power always seems to be a factor in that change.

John, Shelton and Luschen conducted a study of "Race, Ethnicity, Gender, and Perceptions of Fairness" (1995), which attempts to correlate a number of important variables. They learned that "There was no statistically significant difference in the frequency of arguments about housework by ethnicity or race, and women's and men's estimates of the frequency of arguments were similar" (p.365). The authors show that Black men do more household labour than Anglo or Hispanic and are also less likely to view the division of labour as unfair (p.375). The authors suggest some dynamic which the statistics do not reveal may be at play to explain Black men's contribution and attitude (p.375). It might be that historically Black men and women have found employment as domestics because racial discrimination closed off other avenues of employment. It seems likely that the attitudes of both Black men and women are inextricably bound with the historic role domestic labour has played in the Black experience. Also Anglo and Hispanic men spend significantly more hours in paid labor than Black men, (John & Shelton, p.369), suggesting a nexus of other reasons for Black men's larger contributions to household tasks. A

Black man doing household chores may free his wife for paid labor, domestic or otherwise. In many instances Black women may be more employable than their husbands, since females are often perceived as less of a threat in racialist societies. John and Shelton's study remains suggestively interesting but does not really address the concerns about perceptions of fairness raised by Thompson (1991), Doucet (1995), Pina and Bengtson (1993) and Bhavnani (1993). The statistical correlations provided by John and Shelton do suggest new areas in the perception of fairness in household tasks that can be researched.

Leslie, Anderson and Branson's study on "Responsibility for Children: The Role of Gender and Employment" (1991) notes that previous studies suggested "that equitable responsibility would be seen in couples in which wives earn a larger proportion of the family income" (p.208). However:

> That was not the case in this sample. Women in all employment profiles earned an average of 40% of family income. These data suggest the main determinant of responsibility is one's gender: Women are more responsible than are men. Further, it appears that characteristics of women's employment - - in this case, hours worked - -

rather than characteristics of the couple, alter the amount of

responsibility that women assume. (Leslie & Anderson,

1991, p.208)

It seems also that although mothers' child care time decreases as her

employment hours increase, their husbands do not take on more child care

responsibilities (p.208). Possibly the increase in household income is going to

or child care expenses, though "men are assisting their wives when women

need and ask for help as opposed to men's assuming a primary caretaking

stance" (p.208). The authors report that the mothers in their study experience

more strain in the parental role than the men and express the desire "to be free

of the responsibility of parenthood and wanting to get away from children"

(p.209). The men's willingness to take on child care tasks when asked to by

the mother does not seem to ease the strain mothers feel as the primary givers

of child care. Gender roles appear stubbornly fixed, despite mothers'

increasing presence in the work force.

Pittman and Blanchard (1996) attempt to explain the variables affecting

the division of labour in the household in a somewhat different way in "The

Effects of Work History and Timing of Marriage on the Division of Household

Labor; A Life-Course Perspective". Thus they examine "how the pattern of paid less housework oneself, while one's spouse does more" (Pittman & Blanchard, p.88). Further, "Husbands who spend more time in paid work do less housework, but husbands whose wives spend more time in paid work do more housework" (ibid.). Thus we can see that a certain rationalization on the part of wives and husbands of their work and housework duties tends to yield a more equitable division of labour. In addition women who marry at an older age tend to have smaller families and do less housework (ibid.). Husband and wife seem more able, over the course of their marriage and work lives, to reach a more equitable consensus on household tasks as material changes occur in the composition of their household and the course of their work lives.

Matthews, Conger and Wickrama (1996) run a study of "Work-Family Conflict and Marital Quality: Mediating Processes" (1996). They seek to establish both a correlation between work-family conflict and the level of psychological distress and the effect of heightened distress levels on marital interactions (p.63). Matthews and Conger's procedure selected a white rural group of respondents and asked them to fill out a questionnaire. Then the subjects were asked to perform "four structured interaction tasks," and their performance was video taped and "evaluated by trained video coders" (p.66). As expected the researchers found a correlation between job stress and each partner's psychological stress. But "More importantly we demonstrated that conflict from a spouse's job exerts as much influence on individual distress levels as does conflict from one's own job" (p.73). It is interesting that occupational stress impinges on the marriage to an extent that stress from household duties often does not. The researchers find further that "psychological distress influences the perception of marital quality and stability both directly and indirectly by increasing hostility and decreasing warmth and supportiveness in marital interaction" (Matthews & Conger, 1996, p.74).

The study by Matthews, Conger and Wickrama (1996) treats the family as a holistic entity, examining the interactional effects of work related stress on family life. Work stress is itself an outcome of the means by which the spouses earn the family's livelihood, a reflection of the strain the family experiences as it strives to maintain itself at the fundamental level of its economic survival. There might be a difference between the way job stress affects the wife and the husband, for other studies show that the hostility and warmth of the wife has a greater effect on the marriage than that of the husband (Matthews & Conger, 1996, p.74). The study does suggest that a positive work experience has a decidedly positive effect on a marriage on a day to day basis (p.74). The study confirms the usefulness of coordinating data from work experience when correlating other data about household tasks and child caring.

A recent Canadian study gives some cause for optimism (Higgins, Duxbury and Lee, 1994):

> The child care data collected in this study suggest that men's family behavior is beginning to change. Husbands of employed wives in this sample reported doing appreciably more child care and family work than was reported by husbands in the late 1970s. (p.148)

The authors suggest these findings indicate "a value shift in culture toward greater family involvement by fathers" (p.148). It remains problematic to see what effect the recent downturn in the Canadian economy will have on the division of child care and housework between husband and wife. Certainly one would expect the loss of a job by either spouse to have a major effect, like any work-related crisis reverberating through a family's life.

The problem of the spousal division of employment, housework and child care provides a natural arena for feminist theory and criticism. At the heart of the feminist movement is a conflict between those who believe feminism to be inseparable from larger political and social struggles (Rich, 1986) and those employment, household or child care arrangements. The theories of the French sociologist Michel Foucault seem to provide a meeting ground for feminists of many persuasions, as well as for scholars and artists from many different nations. "Foucault addresses the relation between the political and the symbolic in a manner that seems to mediate between formalist, poststructuralist theories of language and marxism's historicized but monolithic accounts of the subject" (Hennessy, p.39). Feminist theorists recognize the need to account for the kind of massive social and cultural change that seems to have left universalist explanations behind: global shifts in demographics, employment, family and gender relations. Feminist researchers and intellectuals strive to advance research and bring women together to act constructively. Foucault's "construction of the subject in terms of the operation of power through strategies of exclusion and regulation" (Hennessy, p.65) has proved particularly attractive to feminism. However, "feminists have for the most part not acknowledged that admitting into Foucault's analytic the category 'gender' as a hierarchical system within which subjectivities are produced requires rethinking the entire Foucauldian project" (Hennessy, p.65). The virtue of Foucault's analytic is that it frees the theorist to operate in the historical present without the static concepts of the past. The problem in his analytic is that it is itself a concept from which Foucault excludes subjects

such as imperialism and racism. Women "have rarely confronted the bearing

this 'oversight' might have on theorizing the feminine subject from within a

Foucauldian framework" (Hennessy, 1993, p.65). Hennessy is here pointing

out only one of the many problems engendered by following through

theoretically or methodologically on the implications of a framework so

intensely involved with the subjectivity of the subject. McGrath, Kelly and

Rhodes (1990) indicate that "logical positivism is still the dominant

intellectual paradigm underlying current social and behavioral science

research . . . [and] it has come under severe criticism from feminists and

other scholars" (p.19). Most upsetting to feminists and some other theorists is

logical positivism's implicit assumption that there exists an objective material

reality apart from the observer (McGrath & Kelly, 1990, p.21). The attraction

to Foucault, Marx and other theorizers of consciousness and subjectivity for

feminists is their attempt to make woman/subject an integral part of theory and

practice. One difficulty for feminist researchers in studying the division of

employment and household duties is the feminist's perception of inequity in

most marriages. Yet most often such relationships are observed and measured by the tools of logical positivism. But McGrath, Kelly and Rhodes raise the question: "if not positivism, then what" (p.20)?

Crosby and Jaskar (1993) review a large body of the literature on the division of labour between men and women in the home. They remark that a great many studies cite interrole conflict in men as a source of stress, but find no empirical evidence to support this conclusion. Reinterpreting the data they arrive at a contrary conclusion, that women in multi-roles function better than women with less roles, and "the degree of spousal support was the critical determinant of a woman's ability to cope" (p.162). The authors next address the issue of ideology:

> We have seen that the conclusion that women are suffering from interrole conflict appears reasonable; but it is not supported by data and it runs counter to reliable research findings. Why do so many members of the media and so many scholars persist in treating the conclusion as justified? The reason the false conclusion has proven so resistant to modification in the face of facts is that the conclusion reinforces the status quo. As long as people accept the notion that contemporary American women experience

becomes, from this Marxist perspective, analogous to the issue of how labor is divided in the society at large. Since we are essentially dealing with capitalist society, the question of class conflict and exploitation for profit looms large. "Women's status in the household makes them more exploitable in the paid labor market, while their exploitation in the labor market reinforces their subordinated position in the household" (Shelton & Agger, 1993, p.38). At the level of simple economics, "it will cost the household less to forfeit a woman's earnings than to forfeit a man's earnings" (Shelton & Agger, 1993, p.39). If in fact a structure of economic exploitation underlies the stress women experience in their roles as both employees and houseworkers, then the context of that stress can perhaps be understood in relation to other conflicts and stressors outside the family. It certainly seems apparent, if only anecdotally, that corporation downsizing has forced both men and women to reenter the work force at lower levels of wages and status than their former jobs. If the rate of real unemployment -- which means also counting those who still have not found jobs after a year -- continues rising in North America and Europe, then the stressors felt by men and women in sharing housework and child care may reach catastrophic levels. There seem to be few studies done on working class families where both partners are employed. One suspects that in an economic recession these families would be the first to experience both the direct economic hardships and the resulting stress on family life.

Recently Mary Maynard has tried to illuminate the debate in feminist research about the merits of qualitative as opposed to quantitative research (1994). She cites the social scientist Alan Bryman who "suggests that positivism and the use of quantitative methods are not necessarily the same thing, as is often assumed, and that there are 'aspects of the general approach of quantitative researchers which are not directly attributable to either positivism or the practices of the natural sciences' " (Maynard, 1994, p.13). Maynard suggests further "that it is not so much quantification per se as naive quantification which is the problem" (p.13). Maynard also points out that many of the methodologies that have depended upon the quantification of data have brought to light facts and statistics about the condition of women, which have proved useful to feminist studies (pp.13-14).

Like Maynard, Kelly, Burton and Regan (1994) acknowledge that quantitative methods are not in favor with feminist researchers, and "that not just qualitative methods, but the in-depth face-to-face interview has become the paradigmatic 'feminist method' " (p.34). Tentatively, Kelly and Burton begin to question some of the assumptions underlying the feminists' reliance on questionnaires, e.g., that women want to share experiences with other women directly; that this is of personal benefit; that it is therapeutic (p.35). They suggest that "The problem for feminists is not necessarily the form of surveys, or the creation of numeric data, but 'the ways in which research participants are treated and the care with which researchers attempt to represent the lived experience of research participants' " (p.35). Kelly and Burton argue that rather than be dogmatic, their "choice of method (s) depends on the topic and scale of the study in question" (p.35).

Jayaratne and Stewart (1991) argue that it is necessary for feminist researchers to have a knowledge of statistics and mathematics not only for their own research but also to critique the research of others (p.96). For example, one safeguard against criticism of feminist research by hostile reviewers would be a representative sampling technique. The militantly subjective nature of some feminist studies does the cause of women little good. " 'Feminist methodology seeks to bring together subjective and objective ways of knowing the world' " (Rose in Jayaratne & Stewart, 1991, p.98). Whether quantitative or qualitative research is employed, the important issue is that the research be free of bias and fair to both sexes (Jayaratne & Stewart, 1991, p.102).

Hans Selye (1976) defines stress as "the non specific response of the body to any demand" (p.15). He suggests that "biologic stress is closely linked to, though not identical with, energy utilization" (p.15). "Therefore, stress is not something to be avoided. Indeed, it cannot be avoided, since just staying alive creates some demand for life-maintaining energy" (p.15). Selye seems to view stress as a necessary condition of existence, a given of human biology. Lazarus and Folkman (1984) postulate that "Psychological stress is a particular relationship between the person and the environment that is appraised by the person as taxing or exceeding his or her resources and endangering his or her well-being" (p.19). It is this variety of stress that the present study will attempt to evaluate.

Hughes and Galinsky (1994) studied men and women in dual earner families and found significantly higher levels of discontent among the women.

They then conducted supplementary analyses within the sub-sample of employed married scientists to distinguish the effects of gender from those of job category. Such analyses allow us to rule out self-selection or lower occupational prestige as plausible alternative explanations. One-way analysis of variance indicated that female scientists reported less enrichment than did their male

counterparts. (pp.266-267)

Another correlation is that women worked less overtime and were less likely to

work on weekends or travel out of town in their work (Hughes & Galinsky,

1994, p.266). It seems that "the psychological benefits that employed women

derive from work are attenuated under conditions of high family role demands"

(Hughes & Galinsky, p.267). There is some suggestion that having a family with

young children mediates the stressors of work-family conflict: "Having a child

under 12 years of age was associated with decreased psychological symptoms"

(Hughes & Galinsky, p.267).

A recent McGill doctoral thesis by Franco A. Carnevale, (1994)

"Striving to Care: A Qualitative Study of Stress in Nursing," casts some light

on the discussion above. In his phenomenological study, which has an

interviewing procedure at its core, Carnevale learns that both his nursing group

in an intensive care unit and his group in a medical unit target the source

of their stress as " 'conflict with physicians,' " " 'complex patient-care

situations,' " and " 'shortstaffing' " (p.142). Carnevale identifies the nurses'

desire to help people, "striving to care," as "the fundamental moral drive" of

his nurse research subjects (p.161). Carnevale explains the nurses' caring and high -- often extraordinary -- rate of competence in terms of Carol Gilligan's (1982) "relational model of human development" (Carnevale, p.155). Gilligan claims that most theories of human development have been based on male models (Carnevale, p.156).

> Conventional human development theorists mistakenly presume that patterns of development observed among men can be used to examine the development of women. Gilligan has indicated that the development of women follows a very different course. She has proposed a relational model of the development of women. In contrast to men, the evolution of women into adulthood is not characterized by the formation of an independent self. But rather, women form an interdependent self, that places primary value on relationships and a responsibility to care for others. (Carnevale, 1994, p.158)

If, as Carnevale interprets Gilligan, the development of women is fundamentally different from that of men and the way that women perceive stressors is also different. In study after study, even though women have relatively good jobs and some spousal support, they report they are still under stress and have little expectation of support at home or at work. Carnevale's thesis seems to support the proposition that occupational and marital relationships are structured more in terms of male emotional needs than those of women. If the human development of females is fundamentally different than that of males, the quantified measurement of perceived stressors and reactions, no matter how discrete, will be inadequate to explain female stress in work/housework situations, or in any other multi-role situation. Perhaps the concept of gender itself may have to be rethought in order to arrive at any generalizations about female roles in relation to male roles.

Certainly, when we consider a woman's relation to current society, Gilligan's (1993) image of the "web" as a paradigm reflecting her relational model of female development is a telling bookend with which to counter the "nest" that Betty Friedan was writing about in 1963.

Theory: A Relational Model of Female Development

Carol Gilligan (1993), In A Different Voice, offers a view of human development that contrasts with that of conventional developmental theory. She indicates that most developmental theory is formulated by men using male models. Conceding a difference in female as opposed to male development, Gilligan says that "women not only define themselves in a context of human relationship but also judge themselves in terms of their ability to care" (1993, p.17). Moreover, Gilligan sees the way that women orient themselves toward others as relational rather than individualistic. She uses the image of the web to represent female relations and that of hierarchy to represent the male. "The reinterpretation of women's experience in terms of their own imagery of relationships thus clarifies that experience and also provides a nonhierarchical vision of human connection" (Gilligan, 1993, p.62). Transpose the vertically aligned images of hierarchy onto the web and inequality becomes interconnectedness. Both inequality and interconnectedness are part of the cycle of human relations. "These disparate visions in their tension reflect the paradoxical truths of human experience -- that we know ourselves as separate only insofar as we live in connection with others, and that we experience relationship only insofar as we differentiate other from self " (Gilligan, 1993, p.63).

Carol Gilligan's description of women's developmental psychology has been considered in the present study's exploration of married working mothers' perception of spousal support in relation to stress, role overload and role conflict. If, as Coverman (1989-a) has noted, both subjective and objective factors have to be measured when studying role overload and role conflict, an

Section Two

The literature review concludes with an examination of four fairly recently published articles that analyze what may be characterized as "the plight of working women in dual-earner marriages". As a rule, most of these women have to cope with an overload of familial demands in addition to a demanding workplace role. On leaving the office or the factory, they know that child care and household chores await them at home. Accordingly, leisure time has to be curtailed, if not totally eliminated. The result can be stress, marital unhappiness, domestic conflict, even depression.

This picture of the lot of working women is confirmed in Marjorie L. DeVault's "Conflict Over Housework: A Problem That (Still) Has No Name" (1990). DeVault addresses the issue from a distinctly feminist standpoint. She claims that the family conceptualized as "a unified group, with shared interests and concerns" (p.189) belongs to the realm of cultural myth. Feminist analysis has exploded that myth, she claims, laying bare the sources of conflict seething within. Essentially this conflict stems from an inequitable division of household labour. More and more wives and mothers today are engaged in paid work outside the home, yet they "continue to be responsible for most household work as well, creating the situation that feminists refer to as the 'double day' for working women" (p.189).

DeVault's "double day" conveys the same meaning as Lennon and Rosenfield's (1994) "second shift". Both phrases suggest the potentially troubled domestic situation that working women are thrust into by reason of a conventional gender ideology that continues to distort male-female relationships. DeVault's irritation is obvious. For her, "the family is a setting where men feel entitled to complain about housework, while women do not" (p.190).

The fact that women almost invariably stifle their resentment at having to perform most of the low-status tasks in the household both angers and mystifies DeVault. For example, women have been conditioned to think that feeding the family is their responsibility, never the man's. DeVault rejects this tradition. She angrily underscores "the inequities arising from the traditional expectation that feeding should be women's work" (p.190).

Initially, DeVault cannot find any explanation why most women shy away from conflict over household chores. DeVault admits:

> I was surprised and a bit dismayed to find that very few of
> my respondents spoke about conflict over the division of

labor: only two of the thirty women I spoke with discussed

any sustained conflict about who would do the work or how

it should be done. (p.191)

But on further reflection she concludes: "Household work is strongly gendered

and ideologically charged" (p.192), from which it follows that "women typically

expect to do housework and men typically expect to be served" (p.192).

Questioning the validity of culturally mandated roles is a difficult thing to

do - for most married women, virtually impossible. Within the home women

will often make choices in order to avoid trouble. One of DeVault's respondents

allowed her strategy to be "shaped by her husband's demands, in response to his

moodiness and in order to avoid his sharp words of criticism" (p.195). Yet

another factor may come into play here, something DeVault views as not unlike

blackmail. "Women who resist doing all of the work, or resist doing it as their

husbands prefer, risk the charge -- not only from others, but in their own minds

as well -- that they do not care about the family" (p.196). As DeVault sees the

situation, nothing will more effectively stave off conflict over the distribution of

household chores than the guilt-induced silence of one of the partners.

The next article is authored by Mary Clare Lennon and Sarah

Rosenfield. Its title, "Relative Fairness and the Division of Housework: The

Importance of Options" (1994), emphasizes its relevance to the theme of working women under stress.

On the whole, Lennon and Rosenfield view employed women who are married as a fairly unhappy lot. This is because they have a "second shift" (p.507) waiting for them at home when they leave the workplace. Children have to be cared for, husbands fed, household chores performed. Moreover, this "second shift" is the product of a "stalled revolution" (p.507), whose fundamental characteristic is thus described by Lennon and Rosenfield:

> The sexual division of labor outside the home has changed
> dramatically in recent years, with over half of all married
> women currently in the U.S. labor force. In marked
> contrast, the division of labor inside the home remains
> largely unchanged. (p.506)

Lennon and Rosenfield go on to explain where the so-called "revolution" has occurred: in the workplace, thanks to the unprecedented influx of married women. But we also see how this "revolution" has become "stalled". Women may be toiling next to men in the workplace, but men have not changed their sex role expectations so far as housework is concerned. For men, housework is still a gender-typed task, the gender in question being female. Men are not, for the most part, unwilling to perform a few household chores; but their involvement always falls short of the fairness Lennon and Rosenfield feel working women are entitled to expect in the distribution of household tasks.

But why has the revolution "stalled"? Why cannot most husbands be prodded by their wives into revising upward their view of what constitutes their fair share of housework? The answers to these questions are provided in Lennon and Rosenfield's systematic empirical research. They write:

> We hypothesize that the lower the income of employed wives compared to that of their husbands and the more they stand to lose with divorce, the more likely they are to perceive an unequal division of housework as fair. The higher their relative income and the greater their alternatives, the more likely employed women are to define the same situation as unjust. (p.509)

For Lennon and Rosenfield, it boils down to a question of perception. Working women who earn less than their husbands are intimidated by the latter's superior economic status. Their intimidation, in turn, colours their estimate of what constitutes a fair distribution of household chores. The more intimidated women are by the gap between their income and their husband's, the more readily will they increase their share of the housework and perceive this arrangement as fair.

And Lennon and Rosenfield contend that husbands, of course, know this, and perhaps capitalize on it all too often when disputes arise. Statistics show that divorce would involve "a substantial minority of women (30%)" (p.515) in unmanageable financial disaster. Their "postdivorce poverty potential" (p.526) is dauntingly high. And, to make matters worse, "only one-third of families receive child support after divorce, and among those the level of support is usually not sufficient to raise income above the poverty line" (p.515).

All of which, according to Lennon and Rosenfield, explains why working women tend to assume a disproportionate share of housework. But the authors do not find fault with them for this because the ongoing reality is that so many women still depend on marriage for economic stability.

But Lennon and Rosenfield feel that women who live in a situation they feel is unjust cannot avoid paying an emotional price. "We hypothesize that employed wives who perceive the division of housework to be unfair will have more symptoms of depression" (p.511). Inequity and psychological well-being are and always have been inconsistent, incompatible, antagonistic; this is as true of the distribution of chores in married households as it is of the distribution of

wealth in civilized society. Lennon and Rosenfield end their article by saying:

> General implications of our results suggest that, because of
>
> their dependence on marriage, women encounter "hard
>
> choices" with regard to the division of housework (Gerson
>
> 1985). Either they define an unequal situation as just or
>
> they see it as unjust and experience depression. Thus, for
>
> most married women this social transition or stalled
>
> revolution (Hochschild 1989; Ross et al. 1983) exacts a
>
> price. (p.527)

A revolution of a different kind comes under scrutiny in an article written

by Samuel Aryee and Vivienne Luk, entitled "Balancing Two Major Parts of

Adult Life Experience: Work and Family Identity Among Dual-Earner Couples"

(1996).

The revolution in question requires us to divest our minds of "the myth of

the separation of the work and family spheres" (p.465) -- a myth whose

existence was inseparable from that of "the traditional family with the husband

as the breadwinner and the wife as the homemaker and child caretaker" (p.465).

For Aryee and Luk, these dominant features of our past social life are becoming obsolete. We have now entered the epoch of the "work-family system" (p.466), which requires an unequivocal commitment to work and family roles on the part of both husband and wife.

Furthermore, Aryee and Luk believe that if this "system" is to be successfully established so as to bring about a radical alteration of existing relationships within dual-earner couples, both the husband and the wife must strike a balance between their working and family lives, committing themselves to both while neglecting neither, the result being an enhanced sense of identity and self-fulfillment both in the home and in the workplace. The concept of balance is central to Aryee and Luk's article. It goes beyond mere statistical significance, especially when the discussion turns to the measures that might help bring this balance about.

Aryee and Luk view married men and women as "culturally mandated" (p.471), the former to provide economic security to their families, the latter to give priority to family and household responsibilities. But this mandate has lapsed, so to speak. It has generated so much role conflict -- especially within dual-earner couples -- that its rational advocacy has become impossible. The authors discern "a growing emphasis in the literature on a balanced view of life" (p.466). Such a view, they point out, entails seeing "work and family as mutually reinforcing, with family experiences constituting part of the baggage that all workers bring to enrich their contributions to work and organizations" (p.466).

Aryee and Luk maintain that men and women's chances of living "a successful life" (p.480) hinge on their capacity to achieve the above-mentioned balance. In other words, they say, let no conflict-spawning distinction be made between the home and the workplace. The tasks peculiar to both must not be subjected to negative comparative assessments. Men and women must instead build secure bridges between the "macrosocial world of work" and the "microsocial world of the family" (p.483). If they manage to do this, they will have promoted "the integration of work and family in ways that will contribute meaning to the lives of individuals" (p.483).

This is a wonderfully civilized vision which, even the authors concede, is not likely to be realized in the near future.

The last article, authored by Janeen Baxter, is entitled "Power Attitudes and Time: The Domestic Division of Labour" (1992). It discusses the moral and economic obstacles facing the establishment of "more egalitarian divisions of labour in the home" (p.167).

Baxter addresses her topic by first creating three main divisions, each of which studies the problem of the domestic division of labour from a logically dominant standpoint. The first division deals with time constraints, that is to say, "the constraints imposed on domestic involvement by paid work time" (p.165). The second dissects the sex role attitudes impeding the establishment of egalitarian conditions of labour in the home. The third examines the nature of the marital power men wield over women, a power derived from their greater earning potential and which they routinely use to diminish their contribution to domestic labour and child care.

Baxter's first hypothesis reads as follows: "As time spent in paid employment increases involvement in domestic labour will decrease" (p.166). This is certainly true of men's contribution to domestic labour, but much less so for women. Men are susceptible to what has been called the "breadwinner trap" (p.166): they choose to do little work at home because so much of their time is taken up with paid employment. No such "trap", unfortunately, exists for women, particularly in respect of child care: "Thus, while for men time spent in paid employment does lead to less involvement in childcare tasks, for women, the relationship is the opposite. Time in paid employment does not lead to less involvement in childcare" (p.174). Baxter is convinced, though, that in a truly rational arrangement "families in which husbands and wives spend equal time in paid employment should divide household tasks equally" (p.166).

But when will reason ever prevail in the contest against sex role discrimination? Baxter thinks reason is virtually powerless, in countering traditional views on gender roles. From a very early age, she notes, "men and women are socialised into gender specific identities" (p.167). Their thinking runs along deeply etched psychic grooves. Paradoxically, women, though traditionally cast in a position of inferiority vis-à-vis men, find it harder than men to repudiate existing sex role divisions. This is unfortunate for them, since "it is the attitudes of women, rather than men, that are significant in altering traditional household patterns" (p.167). In other words, contends Baxter, if the present inequitable domestic arrangements are ever to disappear, women must resolutely oppose them, even if male support is only lukewarm.

Baxter's second hypothesis underscores one sure way of mitigating the inequality prevalent in existing domestic labour arrangements; "Liberal sex role attitudes will be associated with an egalitarian division of domestic labour" (p.167). But how is this "liberalization" to be brought about? Baxter notes that age, level of education, and socio-economic status are all factors that come into play here. Research has shown that older men get less involved in household chores than younger men; older women, on the other hand, actually increase their involvement (p.169). Furthermore, "highly educated, professionally employed men will be more inclined to adopt less traditional family roles than men in working class jobs" (p.169). Baxter feels these are grounds for optimism. Traditional sex role attitudes will be "liberalized" into extinction as more and more young couples perceive them to be unacceptable. What is more, says Baxter, as people become better educated and obtain, as a result, more remunerative employment, they will grow fonder of more egalitarian domestic labour arrangements.

Baxter sees yet another way of diminishing inequity in the household, and that is to reduce the gap between the husband's and the wife's earnings. She suggests that the more you do this, the more equally domestic tasks will be divided between husband and wife. This is the core of Baxter's third hypothesis. It is immediately seen to be intuitively plausible, but her findings demonstrate that it has more than intuition on its side. The author is convinced: "A re-organisation of domestic labour patterns is more likely to stem from women's greater economic power" (p.179).

But can we expect to see this "re-organisation" take place in the near future? Baxter does not say we cannot, but she does think it "unlikely" (p.179).

Improving women's economic status, while a "necessary precondition" (p.179), is not enough, she admits. A more fundamental change is required: "a change in gender ideology" (p.179). In other words, according to Baxter, men and women must divest themselves of centuries-old, inhibiting sex role concepts before genuine egalitarian domestic arrangements can be made.

Role Overload and Role Conflict

Although the terms role overload and role conflict are sometimes used interchangeably, it is useful to understand them as separate concepts. Role overload "is defined as having too many role demands and too little time to fulfill them" (Coverman, 1989-a, p.967). "Role conflict, on the other hand, refers to 'the extent to which a person experiences pressures within one role that are incompatible with the pressures that arise within another role' " (Kopelman in Coverman, 1989-a, p.968). At a basic level, role overload is more directly a function of time: how much housework can the working mother do in a given day? Role conflict is not always a direct function of time, for the main issue is how many different kinds of occupations a woman can perform (job, housework, child care)? The distinction between role overload and role conflict is important because, as demonstrated in the review of the literature, many feminist critics and researchers tend to argue that it is the continual effort in juggling multiple *roles* that is a major factor in women's distress, and not the variety or complexity of the *work* associated with each role. In fact Coverman found in her study "that perceived role conflict is detrimental to women's psychological health, but role overload, as measured by time expenditures, is not" (Coverman, 1989-a, p.980). Thus, whether it is role conflict or role overload that causes women to suffer stress, it has theoretical and ethical implications for the study of women.

In part, the difficulty in conceptualizing role overload and role conflict "stems from the lack of consensus regarding how best to measure each separately" (Coverman, 1989-a, p.969). It seems likely that a combination of subjective and objective means have to be used. For instance, the problem of role overload can often be measured quantitatively; whereas the problem of role conflict is often perceived and measured subjectively, e.g., "When do you feel you're being pulled in two different directions?" (Coverman, 1989-a, p.971).

Conclusion to Literature Review

Clearly the rise of feminism has brought prominence to questions concerning "a woman's role" and the expectation's attached to it. This issue has become a benchmark for monitoring change. Notions of gender equality and the value of housework and child care are at the core of current socio-political debate, but the range of commentary confirms that the writers are still far from agreeing. In effect, Betty Friedan's (1963) "feminine mystique" remains; and how to "read" a woman's personal sense of obligation, entitlement, achievement and fulfillment is an ever-deepening challenge.

Two key images help demarcate the evolution of the "homemaker" of the 1950's into the "married working mother" who dominates the 1990's: it is a long way from Friedan's (1963) "nest" to Carol Gilligan's (1993) "web". But some fundamental elements help us see where problems begin to arise: marriage is still an institution; families are still raised by couples within traditional "homes"; a successful home still requires a great deal of emotional and physical work.

Two other factors alluded to in Section One also serve as constants in any woman's life from the 1950's through to the 1990's, and should help give context to the findings of the present study. First, perceptions are, by definition, relational phenomena (Thompson, 1991). A woman's sense of fairness, support and love received, is derived in relation to individuals such as her husband, children, friends and colleagues (Greenstein, 1996). But it is also derived in terms of her "relation" to the environment, i.e., the larger context of the "times" (Greenstein, 1996). The "homemaker's" sense of fairness in the 1950's was different than the "married working mother's" sense of fairness today because society has been reshaped.

Second, psychological stress is also a relational phenomenon derived from the environment (Lazarus & Folkman, 1984). Again, we may be speaking of either the one-to-one relationship that is marriage, or the individual's sense of connection with "society".

All of the above provides a framework from which to view the four final articles discussed in Section Two.

DeVault's (1990) feminist-oriented "anger" at women's silence or rationalizing in the face of domestic inequity is understandable. But so, perhaps, is a woman's sense of obligation to the "tradition" of marriage. Similarly, Lennon and Rosenfield (1994) condemn society for allowing sex roles to change in the workplace but not so much in the "home". These dissonances should be reflected in the present study.

On the other hand, optimists such as Aryee and Luk (1996) put forward a vision of the modern family as a "team" extending beyond the boundaries of the traditional home, to accommodate all the roles and responsibilities of both a husband and wife. And Baxter (1992) sees a new generation of better educated and more highly remunerated working couples as the natural pioneers of the reorganized home. But both Baxter (1992) and Aryee and Luk (1996) acknowledge the utopian aspect of their ideas when set in the context of a society obsessed with "success in life" through bank accounts and corporate promotion.

Similarly, the researcher feels it is impractical to embrace "utopian" constructs of domestic egalitarian attitudes. But perhaps she can bring an *image* with her as she approaches the present study. At the very least, women need a new image through which their lives may be reflected. Betty Friedan's (1963) "nest" no longer applies. Carol Gilligan's (1993) "web" represents a psychological dynamic that may not be as comforting as that implied by the "nest" image; but in the stress-ridden 1990's, as women learn and earn and strive to "have it all", the "web" image better accommodates the multi-role, accomplishment-oriented lifestyle that has been imposed by society. Gilligan's (1993) "web" is one place from which to begin to view a new kind of woman.

Purpose of the Study

The purpose of this study is to determine how married working mothers perceive the different stressors they experience as affecting their lives. It attempts to discover whether these women perceive spousal support as related to stress and the presence of role overload and role conflict. In seeing how role overload, role conflict and spousal influence play on a married working mother's sense of the *quality* of her life, this study ultimately seeks to present a workable "profile" of the married working mother in the 1990's.

Chapter 3

METHODOLOGY

Method and Research Question

This is a descriptive case study (Merriam, 1988). The research question for this study asks: What is the correspondence between women's perception of psychological stress (in terms of role overload and role conflict) and their perception of support given by their husbands in household tasks, child care, and family nurturing?

A descriptive case study is appropriate in this field where little research has been done to determine the correspondence between women's perception of stress associated with multiple roles and women's perception of spousal assistance received in the home (Coverman, 1989-a; Wanamaker & Bird, 1990; Rosenfield, 1989). The intention is to describe the basic attitudes held by women in situations of role conflict and/or role overload.

Sample

A purposive sampling strategy is used in the present study in order to provide a sample meeting the criteria: working married mothers with pre-school children (Merriam, 1988, pp.48-49). A purposive sampling strategy is criterion-based (Merriam, 1988, p.48). "Criterion-based sampling requires that one establish the criteria, bases, or standards necessary for units to be included in the investigation; one then finds a sample that matches these criteria" (Merriam, 1988, p.48).

Therefore, the researcher selected a sample from which she could learn the most. In the present study the sample was composed of 20 women, all of whom are married, employed and have pre-school children. The sample was taken from three daycare centres, since this is where married working mothers with pre-school children are likely to be found.

The rationale for selecting this sample was that previous research suggests that a significant proportion of married working mothers are directly exposed to stress as a result of combining multiple roles (such as mother, wife, homemaker and wage earner), and therefore should be the best source of first-hand information concerning role overload and role conflict, and the stresses that result from role overload and role conflict (Merriam, 1988, p.49). Moreover, Patton (1990, p.176) suggests that there is a logic to the criterion-based sampling strategy that permits review and study to assure the quality of the research.

Procedures

Three daycare centres were approached and, following an explanation, agreed to participate in this research project. These daycare centres included The Learning Tree, La Maison Educative du Coin, and Garderie Domino. It was necessary for the researcher to receive permission from the daycare centre directors to distribute questionnaries to the mothers. The mothers were assured that all questionnaires would be confidential, and were asked to sign a consent form. Then the mothers were asked to take home and complete the questionnaire. The questionnaires were to be returned to the daycare centres two days later, to be collected by the researcher. A final attempt to collect any missing questionnaires would be made the following day. All the daycare centre directors and mothers who participated in this study were cooperative.

Data Collection

Three daycare centres were involved in the present study. These daycare centres included The Learning Tree, La Maison Educative du Coin, and Garderie Domino.

To meet a target requirement of twenty useful questionnaires, the researcher provided an excess number of questionnaires at the three selected daycare centres, knowing there would be instances where well-intentioned women would fail to complete their questionnaire in a proper manner and/or return it.

At The Learning Tree daycare centre twenty-four consent forms were signed and twenty-four questionnaires were taken home for completion. Of the twenty-four questionnaires, eighteen were returned on the designated collection date. No further questionnaires were returned on the alternate date which was provided for late returns. Of the eighteen questionnaires returned, nine were discarded because they were incomplete. In eight cases, some questions were entirely omitted; in one case an entire page was missed. Otherwise, as long as it was completed, no questionnaire was rejected based on the information that was given in it.

At La Maison Educative du Coin daycare centre nine consent forms were signed, nine questionnaires were taken home for completion. The researcher planned to distribute ten questionnaires. However, one woman informed the researcher that she only understands French, therefore only nine questionnaires were distributed. Of the nine questionnaires, eight were returned on the designated collection date. No further questionnaires were returned on the alternate date. Of the eight questionnaires returned, four were discarded for various reasons. In one case, it was quite clear that a male had responded to the questions which related to the respondent's perceptions of how their husbands behave and think regarding the issues covered in the questionnaire. This obviously did not meet the criteria for the present study. In another case, the respondent was employed outside the home on a part-time basis and therefore also failed to meet the study's criteria - which specified a full-time job. The remaining two questionnaires were discarded because one woman respondent altered the format of the response possibilities, and the other respondent altered the questions. Otherwise, as long as it was completed, no questionnaire was rejected based on the information that was given in it.

At the Garderie Domino daycare centre twelve consent forms were signed, twelve questionnaires were taken home for completion. Of the twelve questionnaires, ten were returned on the designated collection date. No further questionnaires were returned on the alternate date. Of the ten questionnaires returned, three were discarded. In one case, the most important question, which asks, "how do you feel when you have role conflicts?", was left unanswered. A second questionnaire was returned with altered questions. And a third questionnaire was completed but contained answers that were incomprehensible in terms of the specific information required. Otherwise, as long as it was completed, no questionnaire was rejected based on the information that was given in it.

In this manner, 20 useful completed questionnaires were obtained.

Materials

The tool used in this study is a questionnaire comprised of 44 questions. For the most part, these questions invite a subjective response. "A questionnaire is a data-gathering device that elicits from a respondent the answers or reactions to printed (pre-arranged) questions presented in a specific order" (Adams & Schvaneveldt, 1991, p. 200). As Smith (1975) suggests, a questionnaire is "a self-administered interview" (Smith in Adams & Schvaneveldt, 1991, p.200). This observation is particularly pertinent to the present study because the issue of role conflict, though partly illuminated by quantifiable responses, needs to be defined as much as possible by the subject (in this case, a married working mother). The literature suggests that role conflict is very much an issue of relative perception; and the research question in this study is built around "perception".

As for role overload, the issue seems to lend itself to responses solicited by the classic questionnaire structured toward quantitative analysis. Accordingly, the present study's questionnaire also contains some questions inviting objective responses. This small group of questions asks for an objective calculation of the actual number of hours of domestic duties performed by the respondents as compared to the amount performed by their husbands. It serves to expose a contradiction concerning the issue of shared housework and child care, and proves to be crucial in shedding light on the difficult nature of the subjects' perceptions. (See Appendix A for questionnaire.)

Measurement

Twenty married working mothers with pre-school children are the focus of this descriptive case study. The measuring instrument used is a questionnaire comprised of 44 questions.

Some of the questions appearing in Coverman's (1989-a) thought-provoking study, as well as the category breakdown of questions used in Coverman's (1989-a) study, served as a guide to the researcher in constructing her own questionnaire. The category breakdown of questions used in the present study is meant to examine three specific areas:

a) further clarification of the problems of role overload, role conflict and stress;

b) understanding gender influences related to role overload, role conflict and stress;

c) illuminating how widespread role overload, role conflict and stress are.

The questionnaire was constructed to perform the above three functions and ultimately provide a conclusion to the research question, which asks: What is the correspondence between women's perception of psychological stress (in terms of role overload and role conflict) and their perception of support given by their husbands in household tasks, child care, and family nurturing? With perception being the basis of the present study, the researcher felt that the questionnaire should be weighted in favour of subjective measurements. But as Coverman (1989-a) advises, objective measurements are still essential when attempting to measure role overload. Indeed, objective measurements turned out to play a crucial part in framing these 20 women's responses concerning the nature of the stress and conflict affecting their lives.

The 44-item questionnaire breaks down into six question groups touching on: demographics; role overload; role conflict; role overload and stress; role conflict and stress; and role overload, role conflict and stress.

The demographic questions (1-11) reveal general information about the 20 women respondents concerning age, number of children, level of education, occupation, etc.

Role overload questions 12, 13, 14 and 15 relate to the actual number of hours the women and their husbands spend sharing home and child care responsibilities. These role overload questions are measured objectively. Whereas role overload questions 32, 33, 34 and 35 refer to the women's perceptions of how their husbands feel about the work they (the women) do both inside and outside the home; and how the women themselves feel about their husband's work, both inside and outside the home. These questions elicit a subjective measure of role overload. All the role overload questions were derived from the Coverman (1989-a) study.

Role conflict questions 20 and 40 are measured subjectively. Question 20 asks for the women's perceptions of how their husbands feel about doing housework. Question 40 asks the women whether they feel happy in their marriages. The two questions imply a link between happy marriages and husbands who participate in housework. The researcher used her own experience and judgement in forming these two role conflict questions.

Role overload and stress questions 16, 17, 19, 31, 41, 42B and 43 are measured subjectively. The questions deal with the women's perceptions of how busy they are trying to fulfill all their roles, and how much or little they feel their husbands help them with the domestic side of their responsibilities.

The respondents' marital happiness and physical health come into play in this question group. Coverman's (1989-a) study and the researcher's personal judgement combined in forming these role overload and stress questions.

Role conflict and stress questions 18, 24, 25, 29, 30, 36, 42A and 42C are also measured subjectively. These questions deal with the women's perceptions of how their outside job affects their family life in general, and more specifically, their roles as wife and mother. Coverman's (1989-a) study provided the basic perspective for these role conflict and stress questions.

The last group of questions - 21, 22, 23, 26, 27, 28, 37 and 44 - combines role overload, role conflict and stress. One question, 22, is measured objectively; it asks the women respondents how many hours they spend with their children per week. All the other questions in this group are measured subjectively and deal with the women's perceptions of how their diverse roles fit, for better or worse, in their daily lives. Two open-ended questions (28 and 44) allow the respondents further room for elaboration. Guilt and fulfillment come into play in this question group. The researcher used Coverman's (1989-a) study and her own judgement in constructing this group of role overload, role conflict and stress questions.

(In review, the researcher found that questions 38 and 39 were not relevant to the present study. Therefore, a decision was made by the researcher to eliminate questions 38 and 39. Nevertheless, because question 42 breaks down into three separate questions - 42A, 42B, 42C - the questionnaire still contains 44 questions.)

Validity

The context of the present study is the married working mother's ongoing challenge to try to juggle her outside job with her household and family responsibilities. Married working mothers' encounter with psychological stress resulting from role overload and role conflict is seen as an increasing social problem.

The measuring instrument used in the present study is a questionnaire. In order to ensure a total of 20 useful questionnaires, the researcher distributed an excess number of copies (45) amongst three daycare centres, knowing there would be instances where well-intentioned women would fail to complete and/or return their questionnaire. The researcher met with each potential respondent personally to make sure she met the present study's criteria; i.e., a working married mother with pre-school children. The basic goal of the study was explained to each woman along with the procedure for filling out and returning the questionnaire. The potential respondents agreed to participate and signed a consent form. In order to ensure anonymity and thus safeguard the validity of the questionnaire as a measuring instrument, the copies of the questionnaire were distributed with only a number used as identification, and the respondents were specifically instructed not to sign their names.

The present study is entitled "Working Mothers Under Stress and their Perception of Spousal Support in the Home". In approaching this study the researcher used Gilligan (1993) and Coverman (1989-a) as two key sources. Gilligan's (1993) relational model of female development and her accompanying image of the web, and Coverman's (1989-a) definitions of role overload and role conflict serve to maintain clarity in this descriptive case study.

In constructing a questionnaire comprised of 44 questions, the researcher drew on her own knowledge and experience plus suggestions from Coverman's (1989-a) article, "Role Overload, Role Conflict, and Stress: Addressing Consequences of Multiple Role Demands". Coverman (1989-a) maintains that both subjective and objective factors are essential when attempting to measure role overload and role conflict. Coverman's (1989-a) definitions of role overload and role conflict played a major part in constructing the questionnaire.

Moreover, two open-ended questions (28 and 44), to which these 20 women responded enthusiastically, deepen the validity of the questionnaire's connection to the respondents' lives.

Gilligan's (1993) relational model of female development and her accompanying image of the "web" were applied to the overall results. This paradigm lent a pattern which helped the researcher understand and make sense of the respondents' collective "answer" to the research question. Because it *is* an externally applied structure, Gilligan's model also gives the situation described by the 20 married working mothers in this particular study (i.e., the struggle to balance workplace duties with domestic and care giving responsibilities) a generalizable validity which may be applied to further studies.

Chapter 4

RESULTS

Introduction

The purpose of the present study is to determine how married working mothers with pre-school children perceive the different stressors they experience as affecting their lives. It attempts to discover whether these women perceive spousal support as related to stress and the presence of role overload and role conflict. In so doing, it seeks to present a timely and useful profile of the married working mother.

A questionnaire was designed to elicit results that would confirm or refute previous studies on how married working mothers deal with multiple roles. This questionnaire was distributed at three Montreal daycare centres where married working mothers with pre-school children are likely to be found. The results of the present study are compiled from the responses of 20 women who met the sampling criteria and completed the questionnaire.

Table 1 provides the results for all the items on the questionnaire. For all closed-ended questions in the 44-item questionnaire, the responses have been calculated and then recorded as percentages. As for questions 28 and 44, percentages are not possible because they are open-ended questions. The responses to questions 28 and 44 are expressed descriptively. (N.B. In review, the researcher found that questions 38 and 39 were not relevant to the present study. Therefore, a decision was made by the researcher to eliminate questions 38 and 39. Nevertheless, because question 42 breaks down into three separate questions - 42A, 42B, 42C - the questionnaire still contains 44 questions.)

The results of the present study were derived from two perspectives - descriptive and analytic.

Table 1

20 Women Respondents

(Table 1 provides the results for all the items on the questionnaire.)

1. Ages of women respondents.	Age range… 20's - 15% 30's - 65% 40's -20%		
2. Number of children in respondent's family.	a) 1 child - 35% b) 2 children - 45% c) 3 children - 20% d) more than 3 children - 0%		
3. Respondent's occupations.	**Management sector** - 1 vice-president - 1 administrative assistant - 1 programming manager - 1 management (unspecified) **Retail sector** - 2 sales representatives - 1 clothing buyer - 1 buyer (unspecified) - 1 office clerk/sales	**Educational sector** - 1 teacher (unspecified) - 2 educators (unspecified) - 1 special-ed. teacher **Academic sector** 1 student	**Professionals** - 1 banker - 1 daycare owner - 1 controller - 1 accountant - 1 dietitian - 1 interior designer
4. Husband's occupations.	**Trades** - 1 computer technician - 1 tool designer (unemployed) - 1 foreman - 1 butcher **Management sector** - 1 management (shipping) - 1 senior accounting manager - 1 manager (customer service) - 1 marketing manager - 1 project analyst/finance systems	**Retail sector** - 1 sales representative - 1 purchases/sales - 1 sales (unspecified) **Professionals** - 1 accountant - 2 entrepreneurs - 1 actuary-consultant - 2 engineers - 1 commercial pilot - 1 freelancer (unspecified)	
5. Average number of hours respondents work outside the home.	a) 30 - 38 hours - 30% b) 38 - 45 hours - 60% c) 45 - 52 hours - 0% d) more than 52 hours - 5% [less than 30 hours – 5%]		

6. Average number of hours worked by husbands per week.	a) 30 - 38 hours - 10% b) 38 - 45 hours - 50% c) 45 - 52 hours - 25% d) more than 52 hours - 5%
7. Respondents and their husbands' combined annual income.	a) $10,000-20,000 - 0% b) $20,000-30,000 - 10% c) $30,000-40,000 - 10% d) $40,000+ - 75% [5% - only one person earning money]
8. Highest level of education achieved by respondents.	1. High school - 10% 2. CEGEP - 30% 3. Some university - 20% 4. B.A., B.Sc., or B.Comm. - 30% 5. B.A. plus designation - 0% 6. M.A. - 10%
9. Husband's level of education.	1. High school - 5% 2. CEGEP - 25% 3. CEGEP and trade - 10% 4. Some university - 0% 5. Undergraduate (B.A.) - 35% 6. B.A. plus designation - 5% 7. Graduate school (M.A.) - 20%
10. Husband's income exceeds respondent's.	a) yes - 45% b) no - 55%
11. Amount husband's income exceeds respondent's.	a) $5,000 or less - 5% b) $5,000 - 10,000 - 0% c) $10,000 - 20,000 - 5% d) more than $20,000 - 30%
12. Number of hours per week respondents do housework.	a) less than 10 hours - 15% b) 10 - 20 hours - 45% c) 20 - 30 hours - 20% d) 30 or more hours - 15%
13. Number of hours per week husbands do housework.	a) less than 10 hours - 80% b) 10 - 20 hours - 20% c) 20 - 30 hours - 0% d) 30 or more hours - 0%

14. Total number of hours 20 respondents spend on the following:	A Household chores and maintenance - 299 hours – cleaning – miscellaneous shopping – laundry – emergency household repairs – maintenance (mowing lawns, shoveling snow, etc.) B Food and finances - 217 hours – family food shopping – food preparation – tending to bill payments – balancing household budget C Child care - 600 hours (N.B. The respondents do 50% more work in these three domains [A, B, and C] than their husbands.)
15. Total number of hours 20 husbands spend on the following:	A Household chores and maintenance - 134 hours – cleaning – miscellaneous shopping – laundry – emergency household repairs – maintenance (mowing lawns, shoveling snow, etc.) B Food and finances - 112 hours – family food shopping – food preparation – tending to bill payments – balancing the household budget C Child care - 373 hours
16. Husband's attitude about helping with housework.	a) willingly cooperative - 55% b) obligingly cooperative - 30% c) resentfully cooperative - 10% d) not at all cooperative - 5%
17. Husbands taking it upon themselves to do housework.	a) always - 0% b) frequently - 55% c) rarely - 35% d) never - 10%

18. Respondents feeling stressed as a result of combining housework and employment.	a) very - 20% b) moderately - 45% c) somewhat - 30% d) not at all - 5%
19. Respondents having days when they simply cannot accomplish all the tasks they should(e.g. housework, child care and workplace duties).	a) always - 5% b) often - 55% c) seldom - 40% d) never - 0%
20. Husbands feeling that doing housework affects their status.	a) very much - 0% b) moderately - 15% c) somewhat - 5% d) not at all - 80%

21. Respondent's reasons for working outside the home.	a) economic necessity - 30%
	b) desire to have a career - 10%
	c) other (explain) - 60% said both
	    A) economic necessity
	    and B) desire for a career

22. Number of hours per week respondents are involved with their children, caring for them either physically or emotionally.	a) 0 - 10 hours - 5% b) 10 - 20 hours - 5% c) 20 - 30 hours - 40% d) 30 - 40 hours - 50%
23. Respondents feeling that working does not permit them to provide full-time mothering.	a) very much - 15% b) moderately - 35% c) somewhat - 30% d) not at all - 20%

24. Respondent's comfort level with the amount of mothering they do.	a) very much - 15% b) moderately - 55% c) somewhat - 15% d) not at all - 5%
25. Husband's attitude toward respondents working outside the home.	a) satisfied - 70% b) dissatisfied - 0% c) mixed - 30%
26. Respondent's roles of mother, wife and employee conflict.	a) always - 5% b) frequently - 45% c) seldom - 45% d) never - 5%
27. Related to question 26; respondents easily manage to juggle their role conflicts (mother, wife, employee).	a) always - 30% b) sometimes - 60% c) rarely - 5% d) never - 0%
28. Respondent's feelings toward role conflicts (mother, wife, wage earner).	a) non-controlled - 60% b) controlled - 40% (This is a general breakdown to an open-ended question. Please see the attached Description of Role Conflict Breakdown at the end of Table 1.)
29. Level of strain respondent's job outside the home has on their family life.	a) none - 15% b) very little - 15% c) some - 60% d) very much - 5%
30. Respondents feel their husbands supply them with adequate emotional support.	a) always - 25% b) frequently - 35% c) seldom - 35% d) never - 5%

31. Respondents feel their working permits them time to provide their husbands with emotional support.	a) very much - 20% b) moderately - 30% c) somewhat - 40% d) not at all - 10%
32. Husbands show they admire the work respondents do outside the home.	a) always - 50% b) sometimes - 45% c) never - 5%
33. Husbands show they admire the work respondents do in the home environment (e.g. child care, household chores, decorating).	a) always - 35% b) sometimes - 60% c) never - 5%
34. Respondents show they admire their husband's work outside the home.	a) always - 35% b) sometimes - 60% c) never - 5%
35. Respondents show they admire their husband's work inside the home (e.g. child care, household chores, gardening, renovation projects).	a) always - 40% b) sometimes - 55% c) never - 5%
36. Respondents feel marital stress as a result of working.	a) very much - 10% b) moderately - 15% c) somewhat - 35% d) not at all - 40%

37. Respondents enjoy their work outside the home.	a) satisfied - 100% b) dissatisfied - 0% c) other (explain) - 0%
38. Respondents would encourage a good friend to apply for the same type of work.	In review, the researcher found that question 38 was not relevant to the present study. Therefore, a decision was made by the researcher to eliminate question 38.
39. Respondents would consider returning to the same type of job.	In review, the researcher found that question 39 was not relevant to the present study. Therefore, a decision was made by the researcher to eliminate question 39.
40. Respondents feel happy in their marriages.	a) very happy - 35% b) happy - 65% c) unhappy - 0%
41. Respondents feel satisfied with their marriages.	a) highly satisfied - 30% b) reasonably satisfied - 70% c) unsatisfied - 0%

42. Respondents describe the life they are leading (check one in each of A, B, and C).	42 [A] 30% a) routine OR 65% b) interesting
	42 [B] 70% a) always more OR 25% b) hopeful
	         challenges to
	         meet
	42 [C] 50% a) allows me OR 40% b) restricts me
	         to express
	         myself fully

43. Respondents experience sensations such as tiredness, nervousness, dizziness or appetite loss.	a) never - 15% b) sometimes - 40% c) often - 30 % d) always - 15%
44. Respondent's additional comments concerning subjects covered by the questionnaire.	Please see the Summary of Respondents' Additional Comments at the end of Table 1.

Description of Role Conflict Breakdown (question 28)

The respondents replied to an open-ended question about their feelings concerning role conflicts. A majority of respondents (60%) indicated that they are not in control of the conflicts arising from their various roles (mother, wife and wage earner). On the positive side, 40% of the respondents indicated at least a philosophical acceptance of role conflict as inevitable and an accompanying positive attitude toward dealing with it - if not a constructive strategy that works for them.

In general, respondents who reported role conflict non-resolution can be viewed as an indictment of modern life-styles. On the one hand, women report role conflicts arising that are directly attributable to economic reasons. On the other hand, women clearly display their frustration in trying to balance their traditional roles (i.e., wife, mother, homemaker) with their career desires.

These women responded with adjectives such as "guilty", "stressed", "uptight and incompetent", and "frustrated". Their anger and anxiety brought out their eloquence: "I have feelings of being split into too many pieces!"; "I feel like life is going by very fast without appreciating it at its most!"; "I just wish I could stay home with my child!"; "I feel I have no time for myself ! " Sick kids were mentioned as a catalyst to role conflict pressures. As was the struggle to balance housework, kids and husband in the few short evening hours at home after their (the women's) working day.

Respondents who report few or no role conflicts have two things in common. First, they acknowledge that conflict in life is inevitable, and they accept this. Second, they have devised strategies to deal with conflicting issues, thereby mitigating, if not avoiding the problems related to role conflicts.

These women seem to be able to live with and handle role conflicts by seeing their lives in a larger context, and thereby giving themselves some room to move: "I seldom have role conflicts. I logically assess the situation and try to relieve the burden on the weekends. I garden in the summer and find it extremely therapeutic. I'm interested in reading and all natural alternatives. I have a friend for the past twenty years I can turn to in times of stress." "Part of my job requires travel, which I enjoy. But I feel guilty about being away from the family. My husband is wonderfully supportive and encouraging." "Conflict arises in life. We must deal with it, accept it, and not be too hard on ourselves. I try to be the best that I can be in each role I take on. I 'vent' with friends who have undergone the same difficulties." By participating in activities, by working on good relationships with husbands and friends, by remaining aware of priorities and cultivating a positive and healthy outlook . . . these strategies appear to be helping these women cope with their diverse roles.

Whether feeling in control of their situations or not, the majority of respondents were keenly aware of having to perform multiple roles in their lives, and of the fact that these roles are sometimes bound to conflict.

Summary of Respondents' Additional Comments (question 44)

Question 28 inquires about women's reactions to inevitable role conflicts in life; whereas question 44 is simply asking for additional comments to the questionnaire itself. Those women who made additional comments in question 44 appeared to be responding from a less emotional position, as compared to their gut responses when replying to a direct question about role conflicts in question 28. The majority of women who responded to question 44 appear to have come away from the questionnaire and its issues in a rational and/or philosophical manner.

The respondents mentioned the fact that economic realities of the 1990's leave most women with no choice between mothering or working. These women felt achieving success in multiple roles is all the more difficult because there are very few role models in the generation preceding them. They were very aware of the difficulties in making decisions concerning the balancing of home and work; they characterized these decisions as "moral choices". Some respondents even offered socially oriented ideas such as a 3-day work week for working mothers, but they were not unrealistic in their expectations.

Some comments made by the women respondents:

"Quality time with my kids and husband is extremely important."

"I have great friends who act as a support network."

"Loving your job or career helps tremendously."

In analyzing the general tone of these women's comments, the researcher concluded that 25% have internal conflicts over roles; and that 75% have accepted the reality of conflicts in everyday life, and have devised strategies to deal with these conflicts.

Two final observations on the part of the respondents:

"I feel that being a working mom is a juggling act. Work allows me to express myself but also restricts the time I spend with my child."

"Balance is necessary in all facets - work, love, mothering, etc."

In conclusion, the researcher notes that the responses of 20 different women make it clear there is no specific formula for success when it comes to juggling a modern woman's roles and responsibilities.

However, the researcher emphasizes that maintaining a positive attitude is the key to achieving the balance necessary for leading a productive life as a wife, mother and wage earner.

Results - Descriptive

The Descriptive Results section breaks down the 44 questions comprising the questionnaire into 6 groups relating to:

1. demographics
2. role overload
3. role conflict
4. role overload and stress
5. role conflict and stress
6. role overload, role conflict, and stress.

1. The data for the demographics are provided in questions 1 to 11. These are families with no more than three children, where both husband and wife are earning income outside the home. There is a range of occupations for both the women respondents and their husbands which defies any sort of demographic pigeonholing of this group regarding socio-economic standing. There is also a broad range of educational levels in the group of men and women. And there is a general parity between the respondents and their husbands regarding occupation, income and educational achievement.

However, these husbands and wives show an interesting divergence in the number of hours worked outside the home per week. The women respondents are working full-time work weeks on a par with their husbands. But it appears these women are not putting in overtime hours to the same degree as their husbands. In question 5, women working outside the home 45-52 hours per week equals 0%. Whereas in question 6, husbands working 45-52 hours equals 25%. This may be where the divergence in domestic roles and responsibilities begins to occur. Husbands are arriving home after having worked considerably more hours outside the home than their wives, and appear to be correspondingly less willing and/or interested in participating in household duties and child care.

Interestingly, money does not appear to be a factor in determining the husbands' level of participation in the home environment. Question 10 reveals that husbands' and respondents' incomes are fairly equal. In fact, 55% of the respondents stated that their husband's income does not exceed their income. The major finding in the demographic questions is that the husbands' time spent working outside the home appears to be the only real factor determining their participation, or lack thereof, in household duties and child care.

2. The data for role overload are provided in questions 12 to 15, and 32 to 35. Questions 12 to 15 reveal the number of hours of household work and child care put in by the women respondents and their husbands. Questions 32 to 35 reveal the women's perceptions of their husband's admiration of their work inside and outside the home, as well as the women's admiration of their husband's work in both domains (inside and outside the home).

Clearly, the women respondents put in more time than their husbands working in the home. The most outstanding finding is that these women do 50% more work in the three primary domains of household chores and maintenance, food and finances, and child care.

More subjectively, the women respondents indicate that their husbands notice their careers or jobs markedly ("always" - 50%) more than the work they do around the home ("always"- 35%). In contrast, these women report that they offer praise regarding their husband's work inside the home "always" - 40% and "sometimes" - 55%; while they praise their husband's work outside the home "always" - 35% and "sometimes" - 60%. So although these women may not be constantly offering praise for their husband's efforts both inside and outside the home environment, they feel their overall support is more consistent than their husband's support toward them.

Again, the most important finding regarding role overload has to do with the number of hours women spend working in the household domain. The number of hours spent by the women was 50% more than that of their husbands, indicating a severe imbalance and lack of equity between men and women in sharing household roles and responsibilities. This suggests that men's contribution inside the home environment is only half that of women's.

3.　　The data for role conflict are provided in questions 20 and 40. Question 20 reveals the respondents' perceptions of their husband's feelings of how housework affects their (husband's) status. Question 40 asks the respondents, "do you feel happy in your marriage?" The link joining these two questions is the notion of a happy marriage. One would assume that a happy marriage will help mitigate a woman's sense of role conflict; and that a husband's willingness to participate in housework and child care contributes to a happy marriage.

The respondents feel "happy" (65%) or "very happy" (35%) in their marriages. And they indicate that only a small percentage of their husbands appear to be "moderately" (15%) worried regarding their status when it comes to participating in housework.

Therefore, one important finding is that these women appear to be responding to the questionnaire from relatively good domestic circumstances. They are in happy marriages with men who have little problem sharing the burdens of household duties and child care.

4.   The data for role conflict and stress are provided in questions 18, 24, 25, 29, 30, 36, 42[A], 42[C]. The questions deal with the mothering issue, the stress that the respondents' outside work brings to their marriage and family life, and the emotional support these women receive from their husbands.

In this group of women respondents 40% chose an answer indicating that they feel no marital stress as a result of working. But the majority of these women (60%) also indicated a "moderate" sense of strain in trying to fulfill their workplace duties, as well as their parental and domestic duties, and also the role of wife. And the majority (55%) indicated only a "moderate" comfort level with the amount of mothering they do. A majority (35%) also indicated at least "frequent" emotional support from their husbands.

In question 42[A], when asked to describe the lives they are leading, 30% of the respondents chose "routine" as opposed to 65% who said "interesting". Similarly, in question 42[C], 50% indicated that they feel "fulfilled" as opposed to 40% who feel "restricted".

The most outstanding finding here is related to the 40% of the women respondents who describe their lives as "restricted". It stands in contrast to the majority of responses in role conflict question 40 (65% "happy", 35% "very happy") indicating happy and stable marriages. This contrast raises interesting questions about women's expectations regarding "marriage and family" versus "self".

5.   The data for role overload and stress are provided in questions 16, 17, 19, 31, 41, 42[B], 43. These questions deal with husband's attitudes toward household duties, respondent's feelings regarding their ability to always accomplish everything that is expected of them at work and at home, and respondent's feelings concerning emotional frustrations and its physical manifestations.

The respondents indicated satisfaction with their husband's attitude toward housework: "willingly cooperative" (55%), "obligingly cooperative" (30%), and they feel "reasonably satisfied" (70%) with their marriages. Yet the respondents do "sometimes" (40%) feel frustration and exhaustion. When asked, in question 42[B], to characterize the lives they are leading, 70% of the respondents offered an optimistic "always more challenges to meet", while 25% were more cautiously "hopeful".

The most interesting finding is the optimism expressed by a majority (70%) of the women respondents in question 42[B]. Again, this stands in contrast to the finding in the role conflict and stress question 42[C], where 40% of the respondents indicated a feeling of being "restricted" in their lives despite happy marriages and good circumstances.

The notion of "self " remains somehow separate from the notion of "marriage and family".

6.   The data for role overload, role conflict and stress are provided in questions 21, 22, 23, 26, 27, 28, 37, 44. All the closed-ended questions here (21, 22, 23, 26, 27, 37) deal with these women's conflicts between career and mothering. One open-ended question (28) asks the respondents how they feel about role conflicts, and a general breakdown indicates that 60% of the respondents feel they are not in control of their role conflicts. But another open-ended question (44), asking for further comments on the material covered in the questionnaire reveals that 75%

of these women have accepted role conflict as an inevitable part of the lives they have chosen.

Question 37 presents the most outstanding finding here, in that 100% of the respondents describe themselves as "satisfied" with their paid jobs outside the home. This would imply that these women need work in their lives for reasons that go beyond the strictly economic.

The researcher is continually drawn back to the 40% of respondents in the role conflict and stress question, 42[C], who expressed feelings of being "restricted" in their lives. It is as though this small group of women are admitting something that points to a deeper realization. "Fulfillment" appears to be greater than the sum of the parts - wife, mother, wage earner - and achieving it remains a life-long and very subjective challenge.

Results - Analytic

The above descriptive results were further analyzed by grouping specific sets of item results together in order to determine kinds of correspondences between women's perception of psychological stress (in terms of role overload and role conflict), and their perception of support given by their husbands in household tasks, child care, and family nurturing.

Set one (questions 18, 21, 25, 32, 33, 42[A]). These items test the respondent's perception of psychological stress that results from role conflict.

Question 18 asks, "do you feel stressed as a result of combining housework and employment?" Whereas 20% of the respondents report feeling "very" stressed, 45% feel "moderately" stressed, and 30% report being "somewhat" stressed. Only 5% of these women claim to be "not at all" stressed as a result of role combination demands.

Question 21 asks the respondents their reasons for working full-time outside the home. The breakdown is as follows: 30% say "economic"; 10% report a "desire to have a career"; 60% cited "both of the above".

Question 25 reveals the respondent's perceptions of their husband's attitude toward them working outside the home. It is reported that 70% of their husbands are "satisfied" with them working outside the home, while 30% have "mixed" feelings.

Question 32 asks the respondents if they feel their husbands admire the work they do outside the home. These women say 50% of their husbands "always" admire their outside work, as compared to 45%

who "sometimes" do, while only 5% "never" admire their work outside the home.

Question 33 asks the respondents if they feel their husbands admire the work they do inside the home environment. These women feel that 35% of their husbands "always" show admiration for their work inside the home, while 60% "sometimes" show admiration, and only 5% "never" do.

In question 42[A], when asked to describe the lives they are leading, 65% of the respondents answered "interesting" as opposed to 30% who responded "routine".

In set one (questions 18, 21, 25, 32, 33, 42[A]), the pattern of results suggests that these women are seeking out multiple roles for a variety of reasons, and that stress is an inevitable part of the hectic lifestyle based as much on free choice, spousal support and a desire for self-expression as it is on economic necessity.

Set two (questions 19, 24, 30, 31, 40, 41, 42[B], 43). These items test role overload factors linked to the women's perception of psychological stress.

Question 19 asks, "do you have days when you simply can't accomplish all the tasks you should (e.g. housework, child care, and workplace duties)?" Only 5% of the respondents report "always", 55%

say "often", 40% "seldom", 0% "never".

Question 24 inquires about the respondents' comfort level with

the amount of mothering they do. Here 55% say they are "moderately"

comfortable, 15% reply "very much", 15% "somewhat", and 5% say "not

at all".

Question 30 asks the respondents if they feel their husbands

supply them with adequate emotional support. Here 25% report "always",

35% "frequently", 35% "seldom", and 5% "never".

Conversely, question 31 asks the respondents if they feel their

working permits them time to provide their husbands with emotional

support. These 20 women reply "very much" - 20%, "moderately" - 30%,

"somewhat" - 40%, and "not at all" - 10%.

Question 40 asks the respondents if they feel happy in their

marriages. They all do: 65% "happy", 35% "very happy".

Question 41 asks if the respondents feel satisfied with their

marriages. These women describe themselves as "highly satisfied" - 30%,

and "reasonably satisfied" - 70%.

In question 42[B] the women are asked to describe the lives they are leading. Here 70% answer optimistically "always more challenges to meet", while 25% choose the more cautious "hopeful".

Question 43 asks the respondents if they ever experience sensations such as tiredness, nervousness, dizziness or appetite loss. Only 15% say "never", while 40% say "sometimes", 30% "often", and 15% "always".

In set two (questions 19, 24, 30, 31, 40, 41, 42[B], 43), the pattern of results suggests that although these women do admit to a certain amount of role overload, their marital and lifestyle expectations are being met to a greater rather than lesser degree. Thus the researcher concludes that role overload has no significant influence on these women's perception of any psychological stress that they may or may not be experiencing.

Set three (questions 16, 17, 20, 23, 24, 29, 36). These items test the women's perception of psychological stress in terms of how their career or job affects their family life.

Question 16 asks the respondents to describe their husband's attitude about helping with housework. Here 55% describe their husbands as "willingly cooperative", 30% say "obligingly cooperative",

10% report "resentfully cooperative", and 5% state "not at all cooperative".

Question 17 asks the respondents if their husbands take it upon themselves to do housework. These women report 55% of their husbands "frequently" undertake household duties, 35% "rarely", and 10% "never".

Question 20 asks the respondents if their husbands feel that doing housework affects their status. The women indicate that 80% of their husbands feel their status is "not at all" affected by doing housework, 15% feel it is "moderately" affected, and 5% "somewhat" affected.

Question 23 asks the respondents, "do you feel that working permits you to provide full-time mothering?" Only 15% of the respondents feel "very much" able to provide full-time mothering, whereas 35% feel "moderately" able, 30% "somewhat" able, and 20% feel "not at all" able to provide full-time mothering.

Question 24 asks, "do you feel comfortable with the amount of mothering you do?" Here 15% of the respondents report they are "very much" comfortable with the amount of mothering they do, 55% are "moderately" comfortable, 15% "somewhat", and only 5% report "not at all".

Question 29 asks the respondents how much strain their job outside the home has on their family life. In this instance, 15% say "none", 15% say "very little", 60% admit to "some" strain, but only 5% report "very much".

Question 36 asks, "do you feel marital stress as a result of working?" To this, 40% of these women say "not at all", 35% report "somewhat", 15% reply "moderately", and 10% say "very much".

In set three (questions 16, 17, 20, 23, 24, 29, 36), the pattern of results suggests that although their husbands participate in taking care of household responsibilities, these 20 women still feel their career or job does put strain on both their marital relationship and broader sense of "family life".

Set four (questions 26, 27, 28, 37, 42[C], 44). These items test the women's perception of psychological stress as it combines role overload, role conflict and stress.

Question 26 inquires, "you are a mother, wife and employee; how often do these roles conflict with each other?" Only 5% of the respondents report that they "always" feel conflicted, whereas 45% say "frequently". But this stands in opposition to 45% reporting "seldom" and 5% who say they "never" do.

Question 27 asks, "do you manage to juggle role conflicts easily?" Whereas 30% of the respondents report that they can "always" find balance in managing role conflicts, most of the women - 60% - admit that they can only achieve this balance "sometimes". And 5% say they "rarely" find a balance in managing role conflicts.

Question 28 was an open-ended question in which the respondents were asked to expand on their feelings toward role conflicts. These women replied with a range of gut responses, but an overall analysis reveals that 60% admit they are not in control of the conflicts arising from their various roles (mother, wife, and wage earner). On the positive side, 40% of the respondents indicate at least a philosophical acceptance of role conflict as inevitable.

Question 37 asks, "do you enjoy your work outside the home?" A full 100% of these 20 women respondents report that they are "satisfied".

Question 42[C] asks the respondents to describe the lives they are leading. Here, 50% indicate choice a) "allows me to express myself fully", as opposed to choice b), where 40% of the respondents say they feel "restricted".

Question 44 requested that the respondents make further comments on the subjects covered in the questionnaire. Many of these women took advantage of the opportunity to express their views on marriage, motherhood and work in combination. In analyzing the general tone of their comments, the researcher concluded that 25% have internal conflicts over roles; and that 75% have accepted the reality of conflicts in everyday life, and have devised strategies to deal with these conflicts.

In set four (questions 26, 27, 28, 37, 42[C], 44), the pattern of results suggests that work is the top priority for these 20 women, and that although they are experiencing role conflict they are prepared to live with it regardless of the consequences it brings to their home environment.

Conclusion to Results

In conclusion, the Descriptive and Analytical results show a group of women who are very aware of their traditional responsibilities (wife, mother and homemaker) and yet persevere in pursuing careers despite the psychological stress that working outside the home may put upon their "domestic duties". The findings make it clear to the researcher that this is a complex dilemma for these women to face. It seems that these women are asking themselves, "are my traditional roles fulfilling my primary responsibilities to *myself* as an individual?" An ongoing struggle between traditional expectations and an arising impulse to expand these women's lives is the defining feature of the present study.

Although highly aware of their responsibilities, these findings show the respondents contradicting themselves with an intriguing unawareness as they try to express what they need, want and *should be* feeling. They express a desire to work outside the home, although they admit that working full-time outside the home is not absolutely necessary in terms of financial needs. But when they return home to contend with their domestic and child care responsibilities, they feel overly burdened. In fact, as the four objective role overload questions (12, 13, 14, 15) reveal, these women *are* doing twice as much work inside the home as their husbands.

One would expect that these women's perception of psychological stress in terms of role overload and role conflict would have a great deal to do with the role their husbands play in their lives. Their own *numbers show* that their husbands do 50% less domestic work than they do. But the *respondents say* that their husbands are "willingly cooperative" about doing housework (55%) and that they "frequently" (55%) take it upon themselves to do housework. What's more, the vast majority (80%) report that their husbands do not feel that doing housework affects their status. These women see themselves as living with husbands who have a good attitude when it comes to sharing the burden at home. In fact, these women say they are "happy in" (65%), and "reasonably satisfied with" (70%), their marriages. When the respondents were asked, in question 44, to make additional comments concerning the questionnaire, 75% expressed a philosophical acceptance of role conflicts in everyday life.

Still, despite "acceptance" of role overload and role conflict, and reports of relatively "happy" domestic situations, these women complain that psychological stress is a significant reality in their lives. The majority (55%) are only "moderately" comfortable with the amount of mothering they do. The majority (55%) say there are "often" days when they cannot accomplish all the tasks they should (e.g. housework, child care and workplace duties). The majority (60%) admit that their outside job does have "some" stress on their family life. In fact, when they have finished philosophizing about their acceptance of life as it is and describing their coping strategies, the majority (60%) of these women admit they are not in control of their role conflicts. Their responses to open-ended question 28 - which asks for their *feelings* about role conflicts - add heartfelt background to these women's admissions concerning the negative elements of their multi-faceted lives.

But 100% of the respondents report being "satisfied" with their work outside the home.

And a quiet minority (40%) of these women describe their lives as "restricted", despite all the positive words about spousal support.

The findings suggest that role *responsibilities* remain a major issue for these married working mothers. The most intriguing factor at play in this study is not so much the perception of psychological stress from role overload and role conflict, but these women's apparent inability to come to terms with an essential dilemma that shows in their contradictions. It seems these women are trying *not* to admit that their working full-time outside the home goes beyond desire and falls into the realm of existential need. What's more, in admitting to psychological stress arising from role overload and role conflict, maybe these women fear they are admitting not only to weakness and limitations but also to a resentment of the more traditional roles. Because to do so would be *self-*contradictory in terms of Woman as "wife, mother and care giver".

It appears to be a question of expectations imposed by the respondents upon themselves. The "super mom" is doing battle with the "traditional mom". The goal is fulfillment; but the overall balance required to achieve it remains elusive to this group of 20 married working mothers.

The research question asked: What is the correspondence between women's perception of psychological stress (in terms of role overload and role conflict) and their perception of support given by their husbands in household tasks, child care, and family nurturing? In terms of an "answer" to the research question, these 20 women present what one might consider to be an unsatisfying picture of the married working mother's situation - what with their contradictory responses throughout the questionnaire and their ultimately uncertain representation of themselves. To the researcher seeking clarity, their apparent unawareness of their contradictions is frustrating, especially when the findings show these women to be so well attuned to their sense of responsibility. Perhaps Carol Gilligan's (1993) relational model of female development can provide some insight into this seemingly unclear representation of what it's like to be a married working mother on the run.

More specifically, perhaps the researcher can apply Gilligan's image of the "web" - which is a visual representation of this conceptual model - as the paradigm of a woman's mode of relational thinking and acting. As follows:

Gilligan sees the way that women orient themselves toward others as relational rather than individualistic. She uses the image of the web to represent an environment or *community* of female relations. The pattern of a web is multi-directional. The "builder" of the web may be seen to be working in one direction at one moment, then in an opposite direction the next. But despite all her apparent chaotic movement, the web builder ultimately finishes with an elaborate and intricately balanced structure.

Transposing this image of the web "builder" to a woman's *interior* network of relationship, the researcher sees 20 women who are highly aware of themselves as constructors of busy, multi-faceted lives. Reacting on their sense of responsibility, care, love, etc., the wording of one question makes these women respond one way, while another question, formed with slightly different wording but focusing on the same issue, may send them in a seemingly opposite direction. In other words, the "mother" responds in one way while the "wife" responds in another, and the "homemaker" sees the issue from yet another point of view. But regardless of the particular point of view dictated by the role, a relational-oriented psyche, if not mode of thinking, is at the heart of these women's contradictions. Their thoughts may appear contradictory but they are totally involved in tying together the diverse elements of their lives: their "webs".

Thus Gilligan's (1993) relational model of female development appears to give definition to the married working mother's dilemma. As such, Gilligan's model also lends a helpful structure to these women's collective "answer" to the research question.

Chapter 5

CONCLUSION

Globe and Mail columnist Margaret Wente (1997) recently spent an evening with 1,400 professional women who gathered for an event called the Women of Distinction Awards. She summed up this group of working women as follows: "Most of them are terribly time-stressed and suffer pangs of guilt about not spending enough time with their kids. And not one in a hundred would willingly swap her job for a full-time stint at home" (Wente, 1997, p.D7). This is as succinct a description of the modern married working mother's dilemma as you could ask for. Wente (1997) suggests an explanation as to the contradictory nature of these women's situation:

> The mothers' guilty secret is that they *love* to work. And the money is the least of it. Work offers a whole host of rewards, intellectual, emotional and communal, that are not to be found at home in the company of your average three-year-old, no matter how delightful. (p.D7)

On the other hand, Wente assures us:

> All of this is not to argue for one moment that mothers love
> their children any less than they used to. Love (and guilt) are
> hard-wired into mothers forever. Just don't expect them to
> stay home with the kids, even if they can afford to. (1997,
> p.D7)

The present study's findings seem to support Margaret Wente's (1997) observations. Two key terms offered in Wente's (1997) article, entitled "What's a mother to do?", pertinent to the present study are: "work" (outside the home); and "contradictions".

The research question for the present study asks: What is the correspondence between women's perception of psychological stress (in terms of role overload and role conflict) and their perception of support given by their husbands in household tasks, child care, and family nurturing? A questionnaire sent 20 married working mothers in two basic directions corresponding to the two parts of the research question. Questions relating to the first part of the research question focus on the woman as an "individual" with multiple roles and how she deals with these roles. In responding to these questions, these 20 women are clearly *more clear* about themselves in the context of a career than that of a

other words, not all the 20 women respondents fit the collective profile of the married working mother in every aspect, and this is to be expected.

With that in mind, the one finding the present study established with unanimous certainty is that 100% of the 20 women respondents are "satisfied" with their work outside the home. Although they may not admit it, outside work appears to be more important to these 20 women than their domestic and child care responsibilities. This seems surprising. It is certainly problematic. The problem is one of clarity as it affects the notion of "self-definition". Because throughout this study, the numbers imply one thing while these women's words convey a different message. This single 100% finding of the 20 respondents being "satisfied" with their outside work serves as a benchmark. It highlights a disturbing inconsistency and lack of certainty when the respondents attempt to address issues associated with the home. When these 20 women work outside the home, they are sure and confident that this is a priority they love and want to pursue from within their hearts. In contrast, when they respond to questions involving domestic issues they are less clear and even contradictory. Therein lies the basic - and profound - problem with the married working mother's "profile".

The first group of responses described here relate to the first part of the research question. These questions ask the respondent to answer as an individual performing multiple roles.

Each percentage indicates a majority among the choices offered:

- 60% state that they work outside the home for a combination of economic necessity and career aspirations.

- 45% admit to "moderate" feelings of stress as a result of trying to combine housework with employment.

- 40% admit to "sometimes" experiencing sensations such as tiredness, nervousness, dizziness or appetite loss.

- 55% report that they "often" have days in which they cannot accomplish all the tasks that are expected of them in their multiple roles (child care, housework, and workplace duties).

- 35% have a "moderate" sense that their working does not permit them to provide full-time mothering.

- 55% report only a "moderate" comfort level with the quality of mothering they provide; the majority (50%) spend 30-40 hours per week involved with their children.

- 40% feel "somewhat" that their working permits them time to provide their husbands with emotional support.

- 60% admit that there is "some" strain on their family life as a result of working outside the home.

- 60% say that they "sometimes" easily manage to juggle their role conflicts (mother, wife, wage earner). But . . .

- 60% feel that they are "not in control" of their role conflicts (mother, wife, wage earner). And . . .

- 100% report that they are "satisfied" with their work outside the home!

The trend of these responses suggests that although these 20 women are clear about their role as "wage earner", participating as a wage earner leaves them uncertain about their domestic roles, and thus susceptible to perceptions of role overload and role conflict - and stress.

The second group of responses described here relate to the second part of the research question. These questions ask the respondent to answer as one half of a working married couple with children.

Again, each percentage indicates a majority among the choices offered:

- 40% report feeling "no" marital stress as a result of working outside the home.

- 55% say their husbands have a "willingly co-operative" attitude toward helping with housework.

- 55% report that their husbands "frequently" take it upon themselves to do housework.

- 80% say that their husband's status is "not at all" affected by doing housework.

- 35% admit that their husbands "frequently" supply them with adequate emotional support.

- 70% feel that their husband's attitude toward their working outside the home is "satisfied".

- 50% say their husbands "always" admire the work they do outside the home.

- 60% feel that their husbands "sometimes" admire the work they do inside the home (child care, household chores, decorating).

- 60% say that they, in return, "sometimes" admire their husband's work outside the home.

- 55% say that they "sometimes" admire their husband's efforts within the home environment (child care, household chores, gardening, renovation projects).

- 65% say that they are "happy" in their marriages.

- 70% feel "reasonably satisfied" with their marriages.

Thus the descriptive profile of the married working mother, as presented here by the 20 respondents when speaking as part of a married working couple with children, while not perfect, is highly positive.

But as Coverman (1989-a) notes, objective measurements are still essential when attempting to measure role overload. Thus there are also four objective questions (12,13,14,15) which deal with the *actual number of hours* these women and their husbands spend working at various domestic tasks. The responses to these four objective questions (12,13,14,15) indicate that these 20 women do 50% more work in the three domains of household chores and maintenance, food and finances, and child care. This finding shows a clear imbalance in the amount of hours being put in by the husbands in comparison with their wives, and implies a gross contradiction behind the descriptive perceptions expressed above by the respondents.

The work imbalance at home reported by the 20 women in the present study is supported by the Coverman (1989-b) study, "Women's Work is Never Done: The Division of Domestic Labour". "Wives devote two to four times as many hours as husbands to domestic labor. They perform about three-quarters of all the household chores, regardless of wives' employment status, or couples' education, income, or sex-role ideology" (Coverman, 1989-b, p.356). And Coverman concludes that "the more work women have to do in fulfilling their various roles, and the less help they receive from family members or other sources, the more likely they are to suffer psychological distress" (Coverman, 1989-b, p.365).

Question 28 in the questionnaire was an open-ended question asking for "the respondents' feelings toward role conflicts". This question did not induce the 20 respondents to answer from any particular role perspective. They replied with adjectives such as "guilty", "stressed", "uptight and incompetent", and "frustrated"; and with statements such as, "I have feelings of being split into too many pieces" and, "I feel like life is going by very fast without appreciating it at its most". These comments do two things: They amount to a list describing the effects of the work imbalance that actually exists at home, as described by the Coverman study (1989-b). And they accentuate the contradiction between what these 20 women say and what the numbers in the objective questions (12,13,14,15) show.

Some researchers (Thompson, 1991; Pina & Bengtson, 1993; Greenstein, 1996) note that a woman's perception of what is fair regarding the domestic work load often has no measurable relationship to objective findings; fairness is in the eye of the beholder. Reasons vary: the "traditional" values of a stay-at-home mother; a sense of spousal support derived through communication and "symbolic gesture"; a "contract" that is particular to a couple and not to a category or an ideology. In each case "contribution" to family and home is weighed according to a strictly subjective set of measures. In contrast, other researchers (Lennon & Rosenfield, 1994; Baxter, 1992) contend that women who are working full-time, and especially those earning on a par with their husbands, are very likely to notice *and challenge* an imbalance in the sharing of household responsibilities. The 20 women involved in the present study fall into this category. Their answers to the demographic questions at the beginning of the questionnaire show that, for the most part, they are earning as much and working at the same level of accomplishment as their husbands. What's more, their responses to the questions relating to the second part of the research question, which deals with spousal support, suggest that they also communicate well with their husbands.

However, rather than express the "psychological distress" that Coverman (1989-b) mentions, let alone directly challenge the work imbalance at home, these 20 women appear determined to cope with their domestic situations *plus* their added responsibilities in the workplace. The final question (44) in the questionnaire simply asks for further comment on the issues covered in the questionnaire. For the most part, these 20 women replied with a calm and philosophical acceptance of their situations. As one respondent wrote, "balance is necessary in all facets - work, love, mothering, etc."

This is true, perhaps admirable - certainly realistic; but these women's acceptance does not help our understanding of what the married working woman really aspires to and judges to be fulfilling. Their contradictory answers when speaking on behalf of themselves as individuals undertaking multiple roles, as opposed to when speaking as one half of a working married couple with children, is frustrating. Why does the "wife" say things are fine in one breath, then, in the next, admit she works twice as much as her husband in keeping up house and home? What's more, the woman in the role of "wage earner" presents herself in striking contrast to the "mother at home". The researcher is faced with a profile of the married working mother in which "working outside the home" is the only element that is clearly seen.

Two authors that helped the researcher gain a better understanding of the married working mother's situation were Shelley Coverman and Carol Gilligan.

Coverman's (1989-a) study, "Role Overload, Role Conflict, and Stress: Addressing Consequences of Multiple Role Demands", provided definitions of role overload and role conflict which helped the researcher gain insight into the dynamics of the "role" concept, and this helped considerably in structuring the questionnaire. And Coverman's (1989-b) study, "Women's Work is Never Done: The Division of Domestic Labour", corroborated a crucial finding in the present study regarding the imbalance in the actual number of hours the 20 women respondents spend working in the three domestic domains (household chores and maintenance, food and finances, and child care) as compared with their husbands.

This finding - that the 20 women do 50% more work in the home environment than their husbands - was crucial for two reasons. Despite what these 20 women *said* about their husband's willing attitude and co-operative participation at home, it appears that the married working mother's domestic workload is not diminishing at all, regardless of her working outside the home. She may have broadened *her* horizons of accomplishment, but her husband has apparently made little effort to move in the opposite direction - which is to become more of an equal participant in the work at home. As well, this finding concerning the work imbalance at home highlighted these women's contradictions, making it clear that they were not speaking directly to what is actually happening in their homes; the actual numbers these 20 women reported in doing domestic tasks, as set against *all* their descriptive responses, brought the problem of clarity as it affects the married working mother's "identity" to the fore as the main issue of the present study.

Perhaps a woman in the 1990's needs a new framework in which to explore her needs, goals, and priorities as she attempts to define herself. Gilligan's (1993) book, In A Different Voice, proposes a "relational model of female development". Its purpose is to accommodate a woman's tendency to include "others" when she makes judgements that are part of the process of her self-definition. Gilligan writes:

Sensitivity to the needs of others and the assumption of responsibility for taking care lead women to attend to voices other than their own and to include in their judgement other points of view. Women's moral weakness, manifest in an apparent diffusion and confusion of judgement, is thus inseparable from women's moral strength, an overriding concern with relationships and responsibilities. (1993, p.16)

Here Gilligan (1993) may have at least explained the source of these 20 respondents' frustrating contradictions.

More important to arriving at a sense of completion in the present study, Gilligan (1993) also proposes the "web" as an *image* to accompany her relational model of female development. Gilligan offers the web as a visual representation of a woman's tendency to live and develop through social interaction; i.e., relationship.

The researcher *interiorized* the image of the web and found that it served to bring meaningful context to the married working mother's identity dilemma, where the respondents themselves failed to supply strong definition. The image of the web allows a woman room for psychological movement which the more traditional image of the "nest" cannot. A web implies movement - *from role to role*. It also implies work. The married working mother is a fact of modern life.

The values she works out as she defines her multi-faceted life will be established as she moves from one role to the next, and back again, always - by her very nature - working to tie all her roles together. Because there is no definite departure point on a web, it can accommodate a relative sense of self according to a specific role - a tendency which the 20 respondents in the present study certainly demonstrate. The "wife" offers a different perspective than the "wage earner", who offers a different perspective than the "mother at home". As well, while the web is "complete", it is a highly complex structure. The web builder may become immersed in one particular sector in the same way a woman may find herself focusing on her job, or her child, or her husband at different points in her life. This does not mean she has lost sight of the other aspects of her life. She is still "in the web" and working on it.

In other words, the web is a very forgiving image with which a married working mother in the 1990's may identify without losing track of herself and without feeling guilt. If we apply the findings of the present study, many readers might see these 20 women's confident assurance about their "wage earner" role as being to the detriment of their other roles of "wife" and "mother". Viewing these women from a more traditional standpoint - using the "nest" as a model, for example - we might be tempted to pass negative judgement on their preoccupation with outside work, because family would be seen as the prime and central element of a woman's life. But if we apply the web image as a model, we can give these women the benefit of the doubt. They are not neglecting the other essential parts of their lives; i.e., they are not being contradictory and/or less clear about their domestic life because they like or value it less. It is because the "wage earner" occupies an area of the web that affords a different and apparently more clear perspective on a woman's sense of identity than those areas occupied by the "wife" and "mother". But the web is interwoven - relational - and each perspective has an interface with the other.

A definitive "answer" to the research question in a descriptive case study such as this one is probably not possible. Because it is based on perceptions. But a "working answer" to the research question could be: although the degree of correspondence will vary from one woman to the next, in general the correspondence between women's perception of psychological stress (in terms of role overload and role conflict) and their perception of support given by their husbands in household tasks, child care, and family nurturing is displayed in a woman's fractured sense of identity. In many ways the web may be seen as the solution to the married working mother's identity dilemma. The web is where the present study concludes. The researcher recommends that the present study be replicated in order to validate (or not) the generalizability of its findings. The researcher also suggests that any further studies done on women dealing with multiple roles make practical use of the web image as a structural tool; and that the 100% "satisfied with outside work" response, as found in the present study, be more extensively explored.

Because although it may better accommodate a married working mother's multi-faceted life, the web image does not supply an answer to the compelling question: *Why* is the married working mother 100% clear about her outside work, and less so about the home front?

In her book, The Second Shift (1989), sociologist Arlie Russell Hochschild also confirmed (like Coverman, [1989-b] and the present study) that "in two-career couples, women still do the lion's share of the child care and housework" (Lemann, 1997, p.8). Hochschild has recently published a new book, entitled The Time Bind: When Work Becomes Home and Home Becomes Work (1997), which aims directly at the 100% "satisfied with outside work" claim, such as occurred in the present study. This book was not available when the present study was taking place, and the researcher notes that she has not read it. But in interviews and reviews concerning the book, Hochschild presents the issue of women's apparent preference for outside work clearly. In one interview with Mother Jones magazine, Hochschild stated:

> All the data we have show that working women are more
> likely to feel good about themselves and positive about their

lives, and to feel that their contributions at home are honored

and valued - more so than women who permanently stay

home. (Snell, 1997, p.30)

Why?

Hochschild suggests:

Today we have more recognition ceremonies at work, and

fewer recognition ceremonies, so to speak, at home. We're

asked to value the individual at work, and nobody's quite

holding that ideology at home. It's tempting, therefore, to

emotionally relocate to the workplace. (Snell, 1997, p.28)

Thus Hochschild has noted a disturbing down-side to women's love of outside

work. And Hochschild cautions:

But children feel starved for time, and adults feel guilty for

starving children of time. That's a huge problem, not because

your kid won't grow up to be bright and successful, but what

if they grow up to be bright and successful and replay the

same time-starved life that was taught to them? (Snell, 1997,

p.30)

It appears that Hochschild has come into the public arena to validate 20

working married mothers in Montreal who have indicated that they may enjoy work and career more than mothering or running a home. But if a liberal feminist such as Hochschild can speak and write about the negative effects that the modern woman's life choices may be having on society's children, imagine what researchers working from a conservative perspective will do with this issue! Women, and the married working mother especially, continue to be a political focal point. Judith Stacey writes in her book, In The Name Of The Family: Rethinking Family Values in the Postmodern Age (1996):

> The idea that we should all subscribe to a unitary ideal
>
> of family life is objectionable on social scientific,
>
> ethical, and political grounds . . . . families come in
>
> many shapes and sizes, and will continue to do so. A
>
> democratic family politics must address diverse bodily
>
> and spiritual desires in rhetoric people find at least as
>
> comfortable as the ever-popular, combat uniform of
>
> family values. (p.75)

As one participant in the present study noted in her departing comments; "I feel that being a working mom is a juggling act. Work allows me to express myself but also restricts the time I spend with my child."

The goal for a woman is self-definition; identity, realized freely from within, not imposed via "values" from external forces, whether they be family, community, politicians - or even bosses. It is for researchers following in the direction of the present study to continue to encourage the married working mother to speak clearly and deeply about her sense of self from the perspective of *all* her various roles.

References

Adams, G.R., & Schvaneveldt, J.D. (1991). Understanding research methods. New York: Longman.

Aryee, S., & Luk, V. (1996). Balancing two major parts of adult life experience: Work and family identity among dual-earner couples. Human Relations, 49, 465-487.

Bannerji, H. (1991). "Re: Turning the Gaze" Racism, Sexism, Knowledge and the Academy. RFR/DRF Vol. 20(3/4) pp. 5-11.

Baxter, J. (1992). Power attitudes and time: The domestic division of labour. Journal Of Comparative Family Studies, 23, 165-182.

Bhavnani, K. (1993). Tracing the contours: Feminist research and feminist objectivity. Women Studies Int. Forum, 16, 95-104.

Bird, G.W., & Wanamaker, N.J. (1990). Coping with stress in dual career marriages.International Journal of Sociology of the Family, 20, 199-206.

Carnevale, F.A. (1994). Striving to care: A qualitative study of stress in nursing. Unpublished doctoral dissertation, McGill University, Montreal.

Coverman, S. (1989-a). Role overload, role conflict, and stress: Addressing consequences of multiple role demands. Social Forces, 67, 965-982.

----. (1989-b). Women's work is never done: The division of domestic labor. In J. Freeman (Ed.), Woman (pp. 356-368). Mountain View, CA: Mayfield.

Crosby, F.J., & Jaskar, K.L. (1993). Women and men at home and at work: Realities and illusions. In S. Oskamp & M. Costanzo (Eds.), Gender issues in contemporary society (pp. 143-171). Newbury Park, CA: Sage.

DeMaris, A., & Longmore, M.A. (1996). Ideology, power, and equity: Testing competing explanations for the perception of fairness in household labor. Social Forces, 74, 1043-1071.

DeVault, M.L. (1990). Conflict over housework: A problem that (still) has

no name. Research in Social Movements, Conflict and Change, 12,

189-202.

Doucet, A. (1995). Gender equality and gender differences in household work

and parenting. Women Studies International Forum, 18, 271-284.

Eshleman, J.R. (1991). The family: An introduction. Boston: Allyn & Bacon.

Friedan, B. (1963). The feminine mystique. Hammonds-worth, England:

Penguin.

Gilligan, C. (1993). In a different voice. Cambridge: Harvard University Press.

Greenstein, T.N. (1996). Gender, ideology and perceptions of the fairness of

the division of household labor: Effects on marital quality. Social

Forces, 74, 1029-1042.

Hennessy, R. (1993). Materialist feminism and the politics of discourse.

London: Routledge.

Higgins, C., Duxbury, L., & Lee, C. (1994). Impact of life-cycle stage and gender on the ability to balance work and family responsibilities. Family Relations, 43, 144-150.

Hobsbawm, E. (1994). Age of extremes: The short twentieth century. London: Michael Joseph.

Hochschild, A.R. (1997). The time bind: When work becomes home and home becomes work. New York: Henry Holt.

Hochschild, A. (with Machung, A.). (1992). The second shift: Working parents and the revolution at home. In A. Skolnick and J.H. Skolnick (Eds.), Family in transition (pp. 431-438). New York: Harper Collins.

Hooks, B. (1988). Talking Back: Thinking feminist, Thinking black (Excerpts 1-4; 42-48; 55-61; 177-181). Toronto: Between the Lines.

Hughes, D.L., & Galinsky, E. (1994). Gender, job and family conditions, and psychological symptoms. Psychology of Women Quarterly, 18, 251-270.

Jayaratne, T.E., & Stewart, A.J. (1991). Quantitative and qualitative methods in the social sciences: Current feminist issues and practical strategies. In M.M. Fonow and J.A. Cook (Eds.), Beyond methodology: Feminist scholarship as lived research (pp. 85-106). Bloomington: Indiana University Press.

John, D., Shelton, B.A., & Luschen, K. (1995). Race, ethnicity, gender, and perceptions of fairness. Journal of Family Issues, 16, 357-379.

Kelly, L., Burton, S., & Regan, L. (1994). Researching women's lives or studying women's oppression? Reflections on what constitutes feminist research. In M. Maynard and J. Purvis (Eds.), Researching women's lives from a feminist perspective (pp. 27-48). London: Taylor and Francis.

Lazarus, R.S., & Folkman, S. (1984). Stress, appraisal, and coping. New York: Springer Publishing.

Lemann, N. (1997, May 11). Honey, I'm not home. New York Times Book Review, p. 8.

Lennon, M.C. (1987). Sex differences in distress: The impact of gender and work roles. Journal of Health and Social Behavior, 28, 290-303.

Lennon, M.C., & Rosenfield, S. (1994). Relative fairness and the division of housework: The importance of options. American Journal of Sociology, 100, 506-531.

Lerner, J.V. (1994). Working women and their families. Thousand Oaks, CA: Sage.

Leslie, L.A., Anderson, E.A., & Branson, M.P. (1991). Responsibility for children: The role of gender and employment. Journal of Family Issues, 12, 197-210.

Lowe, G.S. (1989). Women, paid/unpaid work, and stress. Ottawa, Canada: Canadian Advisory Council on the Status of Women.

Mackie, M. (1991). Gender relations in Canada: Further explorations. Toronto: Butterworths.

Matthews, L.S., Conger, R.D., & Wickrama, K.A.S. (1996). Work-family conflict and marital quality: Mediating processes. Social Psychology Quarterly, 59, 62-79.

Maynard, M. (1994). Methods, practice and epistemology: The debate about feminism and research. In M. Maynard and J. Purvis (Eds.), Researching women's lives from a feminist perspective (pp. 10-26). London: Taylor and Francis.

McGrath, J.E., Kelly, J.R., & Rhodes, J.E. (1993). A feminist perspective on research methodology: Some metatheoretical issues, contrasts, and choices. In S. Oskamp and M. Costanzo (Eds.), Gender issues in contemporary society (pp. 19-37). Newbury Park, CA: Sage.

Merriam, S.B. (1988). Case study research in education. San Francisco: Jossey-Bass.

Patton, M.Q. (1990). Qualitative evaluation and research methods. Newbury Park, CA: Sage.

Perry-Jenkins, M., & Crouter, A.C. (1990). Men's provider-role attitudes: Implications for household work and marital satisfaction. Journal of Family Issues, 11, 136-156.

Pina, D.L., & Bengtson, V.L. (1993). The division of household labor and wives' happiness: Ideology, employment, and perceptions of support. Journal of Marriage and the Family, 55, 901-912.

Pittman, J.F., & Blanchard, D. (1996). The effects of work history and timing of marriage on the division of household labor: A life-course perspective. Journal of Marriage and the Family, 58, 78-90.

Rich, A. (1986). "Notes Toward a Politics of Location" (1984) Blood, Bread, and Poetry: Selected Prose 1979-1985. (pp. 210-231) New York: W.W. Norton & Co.

Rosenfield, S. (1989). The effects of women's employment: Personal control and sex differences in mental health. Journal of Health and Social Behavior, 30, 77-91.

Ross, C.E., Mirowsky, J., & Huber, J. (1983). Dividing work, sharing

work, and in-between: Marriage patterns and depression. American

Sociological Review, 48, 809-823.

Selye, H. (1976). Stress in health and disease. London: Butterworths.

Shelton, B.A., & Agger, B. (1993). Shotgun wedding, unhappy marriage,

no-fault divorce? Rethinking the feminism-marxism relationship. In P.

England (Ed.), Theory on gender/feminism on theory (pp. 25-41). New

York: Aldine De Gruyter.

Snell, M. (1997, May-June). Home work time. Mother Jones, 22, 26-31.

Stacey, J. (1996). In the name of the family: Rethinking family values in the

postmodern age. Boston: Beacon Press.

Stanley, L., & Wise, S. (1983). Breaking out: Feminist consciousness and

feminist research. London: Routledge & Kegan Paul.

Statistics Canada (1992) in, Lero, D.S. & Johnson, K.L. (1994). Canadian

statistics on work and family. Ottawa, Canada: Canadian Advisory

Council on the Status of Women.

Thompson, L. (1991). Family work: Women's sense of fairness. Journal of

 Family Issues, 12, 181-196.

Torjman, S. (1988). The reality gap: Closing the gap between women's needs

 and available programs and services. Ottawa, Canada: Canadian

 Advisory Council on the Status of Women.

Wente, M.(1997, May 10).What's a mother to do? The Globe and Mail, p. D7.

Wilson, S.J. (1991). Woman, families, and work. Toronto: McGraw-Hill.

Worell, J., & Remer, P. (1992). Feminist perspectives in therapy: An

 empowerment model for women. England: Wiley.

APPENDIX A

QUESTIONNAIRE

1. What is your present age? _____

2. How many children do you have in your family?
1_____ 2 _____ 3 _____ More than 3_____

3. What is your current occupation?
_____

4. What is your husband's current occupation?
_____

5. How many hours do you work outside the home per week, on average?
_____ 30-38 _____38-45 _____45-52 _____52+

6. How many hours does your husband work per week, on average?
_____30-38 _____38-45_____ 45-52 _____ 52+

7. Please indicate your appropriate combined annual income?
_____ $10,000-20,000_____$20,000-30,000 _____$30,000-40,000 _____$40,000+

8. What is the highest level of education you have achieved? _____

9. What is your husband's level of education? _____

10. Does your husband's income exceed yours?
_____Yes _____ No

11. If so, by what amount?
_____ $5,000 or less _____ $5,000-10,000 _____$10,000-20,000 _____$20,000+

12. How many hours per week do you do housework?
_____ Less than 10_____10-20 _____20-30 _____30 or more

13. How many hours per week does your husband do housework?
_____ Less than 10_____10-20 _____20-30 _____30 or more

14. How many hours per week do you spend on the following ?
Housecare and cleaning_____
Food shopping_____
Miscellaneous shopping_____
Food preparation_____
Laundry_____
Child care_____
Household repairs and general household maintenance_____
Tending to bill payments and balancing the household budget_____

15. How many hours per week does your husband spend on the following ?
Housecare and cleaning_____
Food shopping_____
Miscellaneous shopping_____
Food preparation_____
Laundry_____
Child care_____
Household repairs and general household maintenance_____
Tending to bill payments and balancing the household budget_____

16. What is your husband's attitude about helping with housework ?
_____ Willingly cooperative _____ Obligingly cooperative
_____ Resentfully cooperative _____ Not at all cooperative

17. Does your husband take it upon himself to do housework ?
_____ Always _____ Frequently _____ Rarely _____ Never

18. Do you feel stressed as a result of combining housework and employment ?
_____ Very _____ Moderately _____ Somewhat _____ Not at all

19. Are there days when you simply can't accomplish all the tasks you should
do? For example, housework, child care, and workplace duties.
_____ Always _____ Often _____ Seldom _____ Never

20. Does your husband feel that doing housework affects his status ?

_____ Very much _____ Moderately _____ Somewhat _____ Not at all

21. What is the reason for working outside the home ?

_____ Economic necessity _____ Desire to have a career
_____ Other (please explain briefly)

_____

_____

_____

_____

22. How many hours per week are you involved with your children, caring for them either physically or emotionally ?

_____ 0-10 _____ 10-20 _____ 20-30 _____ 30-40

23. Do you feel that working does not permit you to provide full-time mothering ?

_____ Very much _____ Moderately _____ Somewhat _____ Not at all

24. How comfortable are you about the amount of mothering you do?

_____ Very much _____ Moderately _____ Somewhat _____ Not at all

25. What is your husband's attitude about your working outside the home ?

_____ Satisfied _____ Dissatisfied _____ Mixed

26. You are a mother, wife and employee. How often do these roles conflict with each other ?

_____ Always _____ Frequently _____ Seldom _____ Never

27. Related to the above question, do you manage to juggle these role conflicts easily?

_____ Always _____ Sometimes _____ Rarely _____ Never

28. How do you feel when you have role conflicts? Please explain briefly:

_____

_____

_____

_____

29. How much strain does your job outside the home have on your family life ?
_____ None _____Very little _____ Some _____ Very much

30. Do you feel that your husband supplies you with adequate emotional support ?
_____ Always _____ Frequently _____ Seldom _____ Never

31. Do you feel that your working permits you time to provide your husband with emotional support ?
_____Very much _____ Moderately_____ Somewhat _____Not at all

32. Does your husband show that he admires the work you do outside the home ?
_____ Always _____ Sometimes _____ Never

33. Does your husband show that he admires the work you do in the home environment (example: child care, household chores, home decorating) ?
_____ Always _____ Sometimes _____ Never

34. Do you show your husband that you admire his work outside the home ?
_____ Always _____ Sometimes _____ Never

35. Do you show your husband that you admire his work in the home environment, (example: child care, household chores, gardening, renovation projects) ?
_____ Always _____ Sometimes _____ Never

36. Do you feel marital stress as a result of working ?
_____ Very much _____ Moderately _____ Somewhat _____ Not at all

37. Do you enjoy your work outside the home ?
_____Satisfied _____ Dissatisfied
_____Other (please explain briefly)

_____
_____
_____
_____

38. Would you encourage your good friend to apply for the same type of work ?
_____ Never _____ Uncertain _____ Strongly encourage

39. Would you ever consider returning to the same type of job ?
_____ Definitely not _____ Have second thoughts _____ Yes

40. Are you happy in your marriage ?
_____ Very happy _____ Happy _____ Unhappy

41. Do you feel satisfied with your marriage ?
_____Highly satisfied _____ Reasonably satisfied _____Unsatisfied

42. How would you best describe the life you lead ?
Check one of a, b and c:
    a) Routine_____ OR Interesting _____
    b) Always more challenges to meet _____ OR Hopeful _____
    c) Allows me to express myself fully _____ OR Restricts me _____

43. Do you ever experience sensations such as tiredness, nervousness, dizziness or appetite loss ?
_____ Never_____ Sometimes _____ Often _____ Always

44. If you would like to make any comments on the subjects covered by this questionnaire, please use this space provided below.

_____
_____
_____
_____

ABOUT THE AUTHOR

Elysa Schwartzman is an educator with a Graduate Degree in Educational Psychology from McGill University, specializing in human relationships, psycho-social issues and behavioural problems. She has organized and led many adult workshops on parenting skills and on marriage and family life issues, and has also worked extensively with children.